In *At the Origin of the Christian Claim* Luigi Giussani examines Christ's "claim" to identify himself with the mystery that is the ultimate answer to our search for the meaning of existence.

Giussani argues that if we accept the hypothesis that the mystery entered the realm of human existence and spoke in human terms, the relationship between the individual and God is no longer based on a moral, imaginative, or aesthetic human effort but instead on coming upon an event in one's life. Thus the religious method is overturned by Christ: in Christianity it is no longer the person who seeks to know the mystery but the mystery that makes himself known by entering history.

At the Origin of the Christian Claim presents an intriguing argument supported with ample documentation from the gospels and other theological writings.

LUIGI GIUSSANI founded the Catholic lay movement Communion and Liberation. He has written more than twenty books and in 1995 was awarded Italy's prestigious National Catholic Culture Prize.

Translated from the Italian by VIVIANE HEWITT.

At the Origin of the Christian Claim

LUIGI GIUSSANI

Translated by Viviane Hewitt

McGill-Queen's University Press
Montreal & Kingston · London · Buffalo

© McGill-Queen's University Press 1998
ISBN 0-7735-1714-6 (cloth)
ISBN 0-7735-1627-1 (paper)

Legal deposit first quarter 1998
Bibliothèque nationale du Québec

Printed in Canada on acid-free paper

McGill-Queen's University Press acknowledges the
support of the Canada Council of the Arts for its
publishing program.

Permissions
Giacomo Leopardi from "To His Lady," reprinted by
permission of Cambridge University Press.
Excerpt from Part VII of "Choruses from the Rock" in
Collected Poems 1909–1962 by T.S. Eliot, copyright
1936 by Harcourt Brace and Company, ©1964, 1963
by T.S. Eliot, reprinted by permission of the publisher.
T.S. Eliot, "Choruses from 'the Rock' VII," in *Collected
Poems 1909–1962*, ©Faber and Faber Ltd., reprinted
by permission of Faber and Faber.

Canadian Cataloguing in Publication Data

Giussani, Luigi
   At the origin of the Christian claim
   Translation of All'origine della pretesa cristiana.
   Includes bibliographical references and index.
   ISBN 0-7735-1714-6 (bound)
   ISBN 0-7735-1627-1 (pbk.)
   1. Jesus Christ – Divinity. 2. Christianity – Origin.
   I. Hewitt, Viviane II. Title.
   BT216.5G5913 1998   232'.8   C97-901134-5

Typeset in 10/12 Baskerville by Acappella
Cover: *Hauptweg und Nebenwege (Highways and Byways)*
1929 / 90 (R10) by Paul Klee / 83.7 x 67.5 cm
Oil on canvas; original frame strips
Wallraff-Richartz-Museum; Kln 1, Inv. Nr. WRM 3253
©1997 Artists Rights Society (ARS), New York/VG
Bild-Kunst, Bonn

Contents

Foreword

At the Meeting for Friendship Among Peoples in Rimini in 1982, Pope John Paul II stated that "the basic human drama is the failure to perceive the meaning of life, to live without a meaning." He went on to say that this failure indicated a failure to know the totality of the human person's resources – "those of an external nature, those of human nature itself, and finally the supernatural resources open to the person in Jesus Christ."

It is difficult to exaggerate our need today for pondering anew the basic human drama as identified by the pope. Does life have a meaning – in the here and now, and ultimately? Does this meaning have the depth and breadth to make sense of everything: to breathe hope into life's most painful moments and significance into its apparently most trivial moments?

What Luigi Giussani calls "the religious sense" sums up this engagement of the whole person with the whole of life's meaning. Standing in the great tradition of Maurice Blondel and Henri de Lubac earlier in this century, and indeed of literary figures such as Fyodor Dostoyevsky and Giacomo Leopardi whom he often cites, Giussani insists that the religious question emerges from the heart of human experience. Every person willy-nilly poses the question of life's final meaning and destiny, and every person answers this question consciously and explicitly, or practically and unconsciously.

The religious sense thus coincides with authentic rationality and freedom. The most reasonable and the freest persons are those most passionately engaged with all things in relation to what is ultimate – to the infinite (God) that lies within and beyond all things. They are those who realize the capacity to love precisely *everything, profoundly.* All of this is well summarized by Dostoyevsky, when he says that the whole purpose of reason and freedom is to enable "every person to bow down before what is infinitely great. If the person were to be deprived of the infinitely great, he or she would refuse to go on living, and die of despair."[1]

In the present book, *At the Origin of the Christian Claim,* Giussani treats the religious sense essentially in two stages. First, building on his earlier work, *The Religious Sense,* the first volume of his trilogy, he shows how the dynamism of human intelligence and freedom leads the person in the end to recognize his or her insufficiency in the face of ultimate meaning and destiny. The basic human dynamism, in other words, if it is followed faithfully, will open the person finally to consider the "hypothesis" of revelation.

But here a paradoxical reversal occurs: the "hypothesis" by its very nature demands that the revelation of ultimate meaning come from the side of "divinity." Hence revelation, though already anticipated by human intelligence, still comes always as a surprise. And its content is a mystery, even as the mystery reveals itself as perfectly "reasonable" – as the fulfilment of what the heart sought all along but could none-theless never conceive on its own. The human heart now discovers that its movement toward the final mystery had already been sus-tained and guided by the (hidden) presence of that mystery itself.

In a second stage, then, Giussani proposes that this mystery has become a "Fact" incarnate in our midst. His proposal changes the method for approaching the "hypothesis" of revelation, and the change is decisive. "Demonstration" regarding the nature and existence of the ultimate mystery is now understood to occur "by means of a clear encounter with a fact, by means of making contact with an event." To put it in a word: if one wishes to "know" for certain that Jesus of Nazareth is the definitive revelation of the mystery of God – of the final meaning and destiny of all things – one can do so only from within an encounter, a living relationship, *with* Jesus. And Jesus himself permits no shortcircuiting of this method: even the disciples had first to live with him, to experience how he spoke and acted "with authority." Only then could they be moved, and rightly disposed, to ask the question: "Who are you?" In other words, Jesus revealed himself at first only implicitly, in his concrete way of life, which then prepared for the open and explicit declaration he would make in the end.

The third volume of Giussani's trilogy, *Why the Church?*, completes the argument by showing how the Church remains the historical place of the encounter with Jesus.

Perhaps the simplest way to summarize the method of Giussani is in terms of John 8:31–2. Jesus said to those who had begun to believe in him that if they abided in his word, they would be his disciples; that they would then know the truth, and the truth would make them free. The nature of the Christian "hypothesis," according to Giussani, is such that its truth can be seen to "correspond" with our hearts only from within the risk of relationship – or discipleship. We must follow our hearts as opened in the presence of the Mystery of Love embodied in the Lord; only thus are we liberated into the truth.

Luigi Giussani's *At the Origin of the Christian Claim* breathes a freshness and renewed excitement into the Christian proposal. Reorienting our minds and our freedom toward reality in its totality and its ultimateness, he shows that the religious sense is a matter not simply of morality or even "piety," but of an "ontology" that gathers up and integrates every last bit of what is true, good, and beautiful. He thereby responds profoundly to the core problem of our consumerist culture as noted by John Paul II: its widespread suffering induced by meaninglessness and by a boredom that is often frenetic.

David L. Schindler
Gagnon Professor of Fundamental Theology
John Paul II Institute for Studies on Marriage and Family
Editor, *Communio*

Preface

Then came, at a predetermined moment, a moment in
    time and of time,
A moment not out of time, but in time, in what we call
    history: transecting, bisecting the world of time, a
    moment in time but not like a moment of time,
A moment in time but time was made through that mo-
    ment: for without the meaning there is no time, and
    that moment of time gave the meaning.
Then it seemed as if men must proceed from light to light,
    in the light of the Word,
Through the Passion and Sacrifice saved in spite of their
    negative being;
Bestial as always before, carnal, self-seeking as always
    before, selfish and purblind as ever before,
Yet always struggling, always reaffirming, always resuming
    their march on the way that was lit by the light;
Often halting, loitering, straying, delaying, returning, yet
    following no other way.[1]

This is the Christian message as it has been transmitted by tradition
up to this very day. My intention is to recall the profound reasonableness of T.S. Eliot and the traditional Christian message as it originally
expresses itself. This book, and indeed the entire trilogy, is more
discursive than scientific. It exemplifies how one can adhere to
Christianity consciously and reasonably according to an actual

experience. Specifically, *At the Origin of the Christian Claim* is the attempt to define the origin of the faith of Jesus' apostles. Its guiding criterion is obedience to the authentic tradition of the Church. It is obedience to the entire ecclesial tradition.

Luigi Giussani

At the Origin of the Christian Claim

Introduction

LIFE AND THE RELIGIOUS FACTOR

To approach Christianity means to approach a problem concerning the religious phenomenon. To consider Christianity in a way that is not somehow reductive depends on the breadth and depth of one's perception and consideration of the religious fact as such. If, therefore, my aim is to discover how Christianity emerged, we need to review certain decisive features of the religious sense in general. Of what does this religious sense, the religious dimension in life, consist? Or, rather, what is the content of the religious experience?

The religious sense, as outlined elsewhere,[1] is nothing more than man's original nature, by which he fully expresses himself by asking "ultimate" questions, searching for the final meaning of existence in all of its hidden facets and implications. The adequate expression of that level of nature where nature becomes awareness of reality according to the totality of its factors is found in the religious sense; it is at this level that nature can say "I" and that the word "I" becomes a potential reflection of all reality. St Thomas said: "anima est quodammodo omnia" (the soul, in some way, is everything).

This is how for us the religious dimension coincides with the rational dimension, and how the religious sense coincides with reason in its ultimate, most profound form. In a Lenten letter, Cardinal Giovanni Battista Montini described the religious sense as the "synthesis of the spirit." All of the impulses with which nature spurs man forward, all of the steps of human motion – which is conscious and free precisely because it is human – every step man's original thrust induces him to take – all are determined, made possible, and implemented on the strength of this global, all-embracing impulse that is the religious sense. This then represents an urgent need for total fulfilment, for maximum completeness. It is within – hidden, yet determining – and therefore, in every form of dynamism, in every act of human living, which thus proves to be a plan drawn up by that global impetus, the religious sense.

a) A Note on the Word "God." The whole way along the human religious itinerary, the word "God," or "Lord," represents the one object of man's ultimate desire, the desire to know the origin and ultimate meaning of existence. One passage of an Egyptian ode, dating back to 2000 BC, calls on the Nile, as if it were invoking God, the origin of all living things:

> Praise be to you, father of life
> The secret God springing from gloomy, secret depths
> Flood the fields the Sun created
> quench the herds
> water the earth
> Celestial pathway, descend from above
> Friend of the harvests, make the ears of wheat grow
> God that you are, light up our abodes.[2]

Another Egyptian ode, from 1400 BC, is a plea to Akhnaton, the sun. The following passages clearly illustrate how the Egyptians lived the link between "God" and all living things:

> You provide the fruit for woman's womb
> you place the seed in man
> you nourish the child on his mother's breast
> you, lifegiver in the mother's breast!
>
> The chick from the egg still cheeps in the shell
> and there you give it breath so that it may live,
> when you will have given it the strength to break out
> it will emerge, it will run free.
> How many and how great are your works!
> You, you alone are God, there is no other beside you!
> You have created the earth according to your will,
> You alone, the earth and its men and their beasts.

You are in my heart
and no one knows you but your son, the King.[3]

For the believer, the word "God," then, coincides with that ultimate, total meaning inherent in every aspect of life, that "something"
of which all things ultimately are made, to which all things finally
tend, in which all things are fulfilled. In short, it is what makes life
"worthwhile," gives it "consistency," "endurance."

We should note, however, that we cannot ask what the word "God"
means to someone who claims to be a non-believer. Rather, it is
something that we need to catch sight of in the experience of one
who lives and uses the word seriously. I have an anecdote to relate on
this point from my high school teaching days. During one particular
theatrical season, the Piccolo Teatro in Milan staged *The Devil and the
Good God* by Jean-Paul Sartre. I remember that a few pupils had been
particularly impressed by the play and came back to school repeating
several of the sarcastic remarks they had heard about God. I calmly
pointed out that they were deriding the god of Sartre, that is to say, a
god I personally could not hold to, a god which had nothing in
common with what I believed. I urged them to reflect on whether the
god represented in the theatre was perhaps "their" god or a way in
which they found it possible to think of him.

b) A Note on the Question that Leads to an Attentive Search. We cannot
forget that this God – this object that fully corresponds to and satisfies
man's hunger and thirst, the need that constitutes his conscience and
reason – is, indeed, a presence, perennially imminent upon, although
lying ever beyond the human horizon. And the more man pushes on
the accelerator of his search, the faster this horizon recedes, the
further away it moves. This is an experience that is such a structural
part of us that if we were to imagine the life of a human being on our
planet a billion centuries from now, it must be said that it would rise
up within man in the same basic terms, no matter how different his
living conditions might be.

I have called to mind this perpetual situation of disproportion and
unattainability to point out that it is precisely this very state that
facilitates the birth in man's consciousness of the idea of mystery, the
awareness that the object fully corresponding to our existential need
is incommensurable with reason as measure, this need's inherent
capacity to measure. The object man strives towards cannot be
reduced to any achievement or point which he can reach. And the
more man travels along his pathway, the more this unattainability

becomes evident rather than diminishing, so that only the "ignorant" man can be so presumptuous as to believe himself capable of attaining it. If one is aware of oneself in relation to reality, if one is "cultured" in the deepest possible sense of the word, that is to say is an attentive seeker, then one will be forced to face the dramatic disproportion I have described.

This is why, when facing the hypothesis of revelation and of Christian revelation, nothing is more important than the question of man's true situation. It would be impossible to become fully aware of what Jesus Christ means if one did not first become fully aware of the nature of that dynamism which makes man human. Christ proposes himself as the answer to what "I" am and only an attentive, tender, and impassioned awareness of my own self can make me open and lead me to acknowledge, admire, thank, and live Christ. Without this awareness, even Jesus Christ becomes just a name.

THE DIZZYING HUMAN CONDITION

Let us examine the existential situation in which man is forced to live. As we have noted, that "God," that reality which ultimately makes life worth living, is what reality is ultimately made of and its manifestation is the object of reality's constant tension. I, a human being, am forced to live out all of the steps of my existence imprisoned within a horizon upon which a great inaccessible Unknown looms. The more conscious I am of this, the more dramatic it becomes. For, if supreme stupidity is to live distracted lives, it is clear that for stupid people these types of problems diminish. Thus, if I am fully aware, my existential condition forces me to take steps towards that destiny to which my entire being strives, without, however, knowing it. I am aware that it exists because it is inherent to my own dynamism, and I know, therefore, that everything within me depends on it. My human sense, my taste for what I experience, what I approve or what I attain depends on that destiny which, however, remains unknown. This is how the conscious person comes to understand that the meaning of reality – reason's ultimate content – is an incomprehensible "X" that cannot be found through a process of research, through reason's capacity for memory. It lies outside. At its summit, reason can advance to the point where it intuits the existence of "X." However, once it has reached this height, it becomes dizzy, it cannot remain there. Reason's summit is the perception of the existence of the mystery. And, although it is bound by its own inability to know that whose existence it discerns intuitively – its utmost concern, this meaning of all things, this concern of all concerns – yet reason's structure is need to know: it seeks to know its own destiny. And being forced to adhere to something I cannot know or grasp is dizzying: it is as if every part of my being were hooked to someone standing behind me, whose face I could never be able see. To paraphrase what Schweitzer says to the nurse in Gilbert Cesbron's play, *Il est minuit Docteur Schweitzer*:[4] "Do you know of a more powerful absence than presence?"

It is truly a dizzying condition to have to adhere to something whose presence I sense but cannot see, measure, or possess. Destiny, or the unknown, summons my life towards it through things, through the temporary and ephemeral configuration of circumstances. And although devoid of the possibility of measuring and possessing that unknown, the reasonable man is still called to action, primarily to take account of his condition and, secondly, to adhere realistically, circumstance after circumstance, to existence as it presents itself. At the same time he is unable to see the all-supporting framework, the design through which the meaning takes shape. In the Old Testament, the oracle of God said: "For my thoughts are not your thoughts and your ways are not my ways" (Isa. 55:8). This was to remind the Israelites of this very disproportion which existentially cannot but appear as an experience of contradiction. Man feels like he is travelling towards the unknown, adhering to every determinant and every step according to circumstances that present themselves as unavoidable solicitations; since he recognizes them as such, he should say a forceful "yes" with all of the resources of his heart and mind, without "understanding." This is an absolutely precarious, dizzying condition. In the end, man gives in to it, even though he may admit the possibility of a theoretical moment in which he could well have adhered to that unknown which is leading him. Plato provides a good example of this "philosophical" moment, this clear perception of the disproportion between what is human and life's exhaustive meaning, when he discusses the Creator of the Universe in *Timaeus*: "The maker and father of this universe it is a hard task to find, and having found him it would be impossible to declare him to all mankind."[5] Or again: "Divinity has knowledge and power sufficient to blend the many into one and to resolve the one into many, but no man is now, or ever will be, equal to either task."[6]

This reflection of the Greek philosopher is reminiscent of the invocation of the Indian poet, Kabir (1440–1518):

Oh, mysterious word, how can I ever pronounce it?
How can I ever say: He is not thus or He is thus?
If I say that He is the Universe within me, my words would shame me;
If I say that he is not in me, I am telling a lie.

He makes one indivisible whole of the interior and exterior worlds;
The conscious and the unconscious are his footstool.
He is neither manifest nor hidden; neither revealed nor unrevealed.
There is no word for what he is.[7]

It takes just one instant for man to become aware of his dizzying condition, to gauge his disproportion. But the memory of this lucidity does not last.

In the history of mankind – in men of all eras and climes – innumerable examples bear witness to either the disorientation, on the one hand, or the feeling of impotent resignation on the other, provoked by that dizziness, that unbridgeable disproportion. The tragedy-laden lines Sophocles has his leading character say in *Oedipus Rex* are emblematic of this: "Men are the playthings of the gods. They are like flies in the hands of cruel children. They kill them for amusement."[8] And even if we do not envision the enigmatic nature of destiny in such a terrifyingly rigid manner, so many questions, so many doubts remain: what man can attain by his own efforts regarding the divine, the meaning of his destiny, will never lose its image as an insecure, sometimes anxiety-ridden swamp that surrounds him. A phrase attributed to Xenophon has this to say of knowledge: "No one has ever known, or will ever know the certain truth about the gods ... even if he were able to express it, he, himself, would not know it; it would merely be an opinion about all things ... "[9] And, after Xenophon, Protagorus would open his work on the gods with these words: "I cannot know whether the gods exist or whether they do not. I cannot know what form they take for there are numerous obstacles on the road to such wisdom: the obscurity of the question and the brevity of human life."[10] Did not this same sense of disorientation emerge, albeit tempered by a flash of initial trust, centuries later and in a completely different environment in the following prayer of the seventeenth-century Indian religious poet, Taukaram:

My God, must I still explain myself? Do you not know everything about me? Make up your mind! I will be here. My spirit limps and I know of no cure except that of laying my life at your feet for ever. Enjoyment, renunciation are evils: what should I renounce, what should I keep? I have never been able to make up my mind.
When a child in the forest loses his mother and cannot find her anywhere, then, O Viththal, he cries.[11]

The figure of Abraham looms large in this context. The Bible tells us that when the Unknown, which had revealed himself to Abraham through the promise of many offspring, asked him to kill his son, the gift he had received as the initial fulfilment of that promise – when the Unknown with all of the force of his mysterious, challenging designs, asked this of the patriarch – Abraham answered: "Here I am." And so, that strange morning, he set out with his son towards a place he did not know, for an unknown reason, ready to make the sacrifice wherever God indicated, which, by God's will, he would not, in the end, have to make.[12] In that moment, Abraham is a paradigm of the drama of man in his full stature, of man set in that vertigo, pulled into the whirlwind in which the Mystery envelops him. It is a dizziness man normally tries to forget, a whirlwind the ordinary man cannot withstand.

REASON IN SEARCH OF A SOLUTION

How, then, unguided in this forest, can we reach the goal? According to St Thomas, in the history of human reason only a handful of great figures, after much labour and not without serious errors, has only ever grasped some of the truth of the divine. Yet an impulse which is part of its structure spurs reason to search for a solution. Indeed, reason's very nature implies that a solution exists. In a memorable passage from the *Dialogues*, the stoic Epithet says:

Give thanks to the gods for placing you above all those things which, as they have arranged, do not depend on you and thank them that they have made you responsible only for those things which do depend on you ... If we were intelligent, what else should we do in public and in private but sing to the divinity, rejoice and list all the blessings bestowed on us? ... Well? Since most of you choose to be blind, is there not a need for someone who will raise the hymn, the hymn of praise to God on your behalf and in everyone's name? If I were a nightingale, I would do the work of the nightingale; if I were a swan, the work of the swan. But I am a being with reason so I must praise God: that is my task.[13]

Throughout history, man has shown that he has perceived this sense of primordial disproportion, shouted it out, modulating it in different accents. However, he has also proved that he cannot re-member it in his daily life. The desire to bend destiny to our own will always takes over. It is an urge to establish meaning and value as we would like them to be.

1 The Religious Creativity of Man

Faced with the ultimate enigma, man has sought to imagine, to define such a mystery in relation to himself, to conceive, therefore, of a way of relating to it, and to express all of the aesthetic reflexes aroused by his imagination of the Ultimate.

In his celebrated analysis of the various forms of the religious experience, the theologian and religious historian Rudolf Otto highlights the phases and content of that experience: the sense of a created being in the presence of the *mysterium tremendum* and *fascinans* expressed by the words *qadosh, hagios, sacer*. In this approach, man intuits a first facet of the sacred, the *numen*, the numinous essence, the *anyad eva*, the "Totally Other." This first discovery leads to a second, the discovery of *sanctum*, the numinous value which is the second facet of the sacred in whose presence the profane appears to be a non-value and sin an anti-value. Here lies the origin of religion, which is essentially man's relationship with the sacred found to be numinous and to be numinous value.[1]

This human effort, which we have called imagination, strictly depends on the link with reality and it is, therefore, an expression, a reasonable expression. In his *History of Religious Ideas*, Mircea Eliade writes:

It is difficult to imagine how the human mind could function without the conviction that there is something irreducibly *real* in the world; and it is impossible to imagine how consciousness could appear without conferring a *meaning* on man's impulses and experiences. Consciousness of a real and meaningful world is intimately connected with the discovery of the sacred. Through experience of the sacred, the human mind has perceived the difference between what reveals itself as being real, powerful, rich, and meaningful and what lacks these qualities, that is, the chaotic and dangerous flux of things, their fortuitous and senseless appearances and disappearances. In short, the "sacred" is an element in the structure of consciousness and not a stage in the history of consciousness.[2]

In all ages, then, and with good reason, it might be said, man has sought to imagine the relationship linking the ephemeral moment of his existence and its entire global meaning. Every man, without exception, formulates an answer in some way, even without giving it thought, to the question regarding what ultimately constitutes him. And this "imagination" is a work of reason's natural dynamism and therefore a fruit and an expression that is affected by the person's cultural environment. "Etymologically," Eliade reminds us, "imagination is related to both *imago*, 'a representation or imitation' and *imitor*, 'to imitate or reproduce.' And for once, etymology is in accord with both psychological realities and spiritual truth. The imagination *imitates* the exemplary models – the Images – reproduces, reactualizes and repeats them without end. To have imagination means to be able to see the world in its totality, for the power and the mission of the Images is to *show* all that remains refractory to the concept."[3]

Religion, then, is the entire expression of this imaginative effort, which is reasonable in its impulse and true because of the richness it can draw upon, even though it also can degenerate into distraction and will to possess the *mysterium tremendum*. It is an expressive complex – conceptual, practical, and ritualistic – that depends not only on individual personal temperament, but also tradition, environment, and a given moment in history. Every man, by the very fact that he exists, makes a personal effort to identify, to imagine that which gives meaning. Any religion depends on people's temperament, their environment, and their particular historical moment.

In theory, anyone could create his own religion. But according to the natural course of life, there is one creative role in society: the role of the genius. No one expresses what is felt by a society better than the genius in its midst, who has been given an eminently social charism. Most people feel that the creative work of a genius expresses what they feel better than they themselves could express it. This is why we feel that our melancholy is so much better represented in the cadenzas of Chopin or the poetry of Leopardi than if we ourselves were to set it down in notes or words. In human history, the religious genius attracts persons by expressing the gifts of his people better than anyone else. He attracts those who, sharing his historical and cultural environment, feel that he brings to the fore the dynamisms of their own enquiry into the Unknown.

SOME ATTITUDES OF RELIGIOUS CONSTRUCTIVENESS

At no time in his history has man, at the summit of reason's perception of the mystery, been able to withstand for long the dizziness arising from such an intuition. Unable to build in such a totally precarious situation – which is that of facing life before the ultimate enigma – man appears to seek a terrain in accordance with his own measure, where his creativity may construct the "place" for his relationship with the mystery. From pre-historic times until today, man has left along his pathway innumerable traces of this creativity, and I would like to evoke just a few of them as a reminder of the richness and depths of these human efforts (richness and depths whose realizations we do not intend to make an inventory of nor analyze in detail). Therefore, we will merely mention some of them in order to illustrate their original attitude.

The identification of the way man places himself in front of the mystery is the fruit of reflection upon religious experience. In trying to point out what was hinted at before, I feel that the comments of the eminent scholar of Egyptian religion, Siegfried Morenz, are significant: "While engaged upon this work I realized that one has to have experienced oneself the meaning of religion and of God if one is to interpret from the sources the relationship between God and man in an age remote from our own. But one also realizes that the great, simple concerns of mankind are the same through all eternity, whatever variations are induced by physical circumstances and differences of mental outlook. One further perceives that preoccupation with a particular religious creed may open up avenues for an understanding of religion as such ... "[4]

It is for this reason that the following quotations will not be chronological, as their insights into the characteristic forms of religious constructiveness are also valid for experiences born of different circumstances.

When faced with the mystery he perceives as the determining factor of his life, man recognizes his power, and since he cannot bear to entrust himself *sine glossa* to an Unknown, he tries to imagine it in relation to himself, according to his own terms.

1) Man "does not know," and strives to establish a relationship based upon bartering.

a) An initial expression of this attitude is when man feels he should become immersed in the harmonious flow of the cosmos and history. Thus he pursues his destiny by following the rules of that harmony which he surmises is driven by its own inner strength, and imagines the mystery to be the origin and result of the natural harmony he seeks to obey.

Significant among the divinities venerated in the state of Wei is the emergence of one in particular which is evoked for the first time in the year 238 under the second emperor. A close translation of its name is: "breath of the highest peak and focal harmony." In this case, however, we do not have before us a god of any kind ... it is rather a principle, born of speculation on the birth and the formation of the universe ... It is the primary foundation of all being – the first breath ... The appearance of this divinity in official sacrifices as the origin and primary cause of all the forces of nature, like the seasons, heat and cold, sun and moon, flood and drought, signifies the decisive entry of the philosophy of the time into the sphere of the state religion.[5]

Another example, also from China, illustrates man's attitude when he tries to penetrate what he cannot come to know by postulating an harmonious accord with it, an arrangement he would be able to "manage":

The humanity active on earth was, therefore, just a part of a bigger whole guided and controlled by the other part – that which had become a magically active presence. The relationships between the living and these "spirits" with their powerful "god supreme" (Shang-ti) were not at all like the relationships there might be with unapproachable divinities of a different nature. They were, rather, the relationships that might exist with venerable relatives who had definitively passed over to another type of existence but who, in the final analysis, were the same beings they had been before. There was a willingness to submit to the guidance of these "spirits," given that, according to nature it was necessary that they should be readily supportive of the lives of their descendants.[6]

In the even more "distant" world of the Sumerians, we find another example of man's desire to transform the Unknown into Harmony and to imagine a hypothetical world governed by it, whose laws he could study just as he would any other law:

The Sumerian texts often record a word which proves to be of capital importance in religious thinking: this word is *me*. The Sumerians translated it in four ways: divine decrees; resolutions; models; divine forces. Rosengarten suggests another translation: directives. The directives are just, sublime, fruitful; they represent a common denominator which will harmonize the action of all the gods in the world ... The Sumerians see the cosmos as universally governed, beautiful and good. All destinies are charted by the gods. The gods An, Enlil, Enki declare the *me* ... the *me* constitute a bond between the gods and the cosmos in order to keep the cosmos within the bounds of the harmonious reality of its existence.[7]

b) The second expression assumes the more definite appearance of a mutual exchange, a pact, a contract between the imagined powers that guide the world and man, who seeks to give meaning and effectiveness to his own moment in history.

An analysis of the texts allows us to grasp the nature of the sacred among the Hittites ... Sacredness derives from the divinity presented as luminous. The luminous splendour of the divinity is such that it transcends the human condition but not the cosmos. Harmony by contract disciplined the relationship between the gods and men. Men had to fulfill the wishes of the gods. Man is the servant of the gods. In human terms, therefore, sacredness entailed entering into a relationship: man must be able to approach the gods. So, mediation is required. Intervention by consecrated personages is indispensable: they and only they truly know how to approach the divinity.[8]

By contrast, much of the Greek religious imagination has bequeathed a vision where negotiation with the gods is impossible.

Judged from the Judeo-Christian point of view, Greek religion seems to take form under the sign of pessimism: human existence is by definition ephemeral and burdened with cares. Homer compares man to the "leaves that the wind scatters on the ground" (*Iliad* 6. 146 ff.). The comparison is taken up again by the poet Mimnermus of Colophon (seventh century) in his long enumeration of evils: poverty, disease, mourning, old age, etc. "He is not a man to whom Zeus does not send a thousand ills." For his contemporary, Simonides, men are "creatures of a day," living like cattle, "not knowing by what road god will lead each of us to our destiny" ... man is not *stricto sensu*, the "creature" of a divinity (an idea held by many archaic traditions and by the three monotheisms); hence he does not dare to hope that his prayers can establish a certain intimacy with the gods.[9]

On the other hand, the *do ut des* the ancient Romans formulated to discipline their relationship with the mystery of destiny is somewhat different. It is, nevertheless, intimately bound to the need for man's action in the world and in history to be efficient. And,

"Huguette Fugier concludes that for the Roman, the sacred basically constituted the very dimension of what was real: *sancire* was the equivalent of conferring reality and existence, of giving what was real a structure. So for the Roman, the sacred is a mental instrument which allows him to organize the world and find his place in it ... The *religio*, founded on the notions of *sacer* and *sanctus*, allows the universe to be structured and establishes how the relationships between men and the gods will function."[10]

These albeit few examples of the way man attempts to become familiar with the *mysterium tremendum*, testify to the striking urgency, the spur to "develop, as a necessity, the concept that God and man have mutual claims upon each other, that service is rendered in the expectation of some other service in return."[11]

2) Man "does not know," but wagers on the goodwill of the Other when, already trusting, he turns to him.

The attitude of the ancient Egyptian is emblematically bipolar. We have already mentioned the "do ut des" version whereby "God (and what is connected with him) is 'Totally Other,' that which is powerful in every respect and therefore also dangerous. Contact with this 'Other' necessitates strict precautions ..."[12] But "in the reciprocal service relationship, in Egypt as elsewhere, gratitude and piety go hand in hand with hopeful expectation ... Along with *do ut des* we have *do quia dedisti*."[13] A particularly significant example of this trusting disposition is to be found in the hymns to Amon Leyden. Here "what emerges from all this is that in Amon the national cult and popular piety were combined in an exemplary fashion. He was both a political factor and the friend of the common man."[14] The following is an eloquent extract from one of these hymns: "To him belong eyes as well as ears wherever he goes, for the benefit of him whom he loves. Hearing the prayers (*snmh*) of him who summons him, coming from afar in the completion of a moment for him who calls to him."[15]

In a similar vein, both the Koran, the sacred text of Moslems, as well as Moslem liturgy begin with an emphasis on trust in a mystery that succours: "In the name of the merciful and benign God." Another version begins: "In the name of the indulgent and merciful God." Some of the oldest passages of the Koran are an admirable expression of this trusting conviction that God cares for his "own" creation.

> Your God did not abandon you, nor does he despise you
> and the next life will be lovelier than the first

and it will give you God, and this will gladden you.
(But he has already shown his grace to you in this life)
Did he not find you orphaned and give you shelter?
Did he not find you lost and show you the Way?
Did he not find you poor and give you an abundance of wealth?[16]

And, in the context of Israel's religion, how can we forget that splendid prophetic text of Hosea which the Christian tradition also adopted? Here the prophet proclaims total trust in divine kindness when he has the God of Israel declare:

When Israel was a child I loved him,
and out of Egypt I called my son.
The more I called them,
the more they went away from me;
they kept sacrificing to the Baals,
and burning incense to idols.

Yet it was I who taught Ephraim to walk,
I took them up in my arms,
but they did not know
that I healed them.
I led them with cords of compassion,
with the bonds of love,
and I became to them as one
who eases the yoke on their jaws
and I bent down to them and fed them. (Hos. 11:1–4)

I would like to close this brief reflection on religious creativity by considering the dignity of this human effort. Every human being feels an inevitable need to seek the ultimate, definitive, absolute meaning of his contingent moment. Moreover, every religious construction reflects the fact that every man makes his own best effort, and it is precisely this one valuable thing that all religious accomplishments have in common: the attempt. They vary only in their expression which depends on many elements. However, the differences never mar the value of this endeavour.

Through the writings of Mircea Eliade, I would like to introduce a mythical tale at the root of European culture:

We refer to an episode in the legend of Parsifal and the Fisher King, concerning the mysterious malady that paralyzed the old King who held the secret of the Graal. It was not he alone who suffered; everything around him was falling into ruins, crumbling away – the palace, the towers and the gardens. Animals no longer bred, trees bore no more fruit, the springs were drying up. Many doctors had tried to cure the Fisher King, all without the least success. The knights were arriving there day and night, each of them asking first of all for news of the King's health. But one knight – poor, unknown and even slightly ridiculous – took the liberty of disregarding ceremony and politeness: his name was Parsifal. Paying no attention to courtly custom, he made straight for the King and, addressing him without any preamble, asked: "Where is the Graal?" In that very instant, everything is transformed: the King rises from his bed of suffering, the rivers and fountains flow once more, vegetation grows again, and the castle is miraculously restored. Those few words of Parsifal had been enough to regenerate the whole of nature. But those few words propound the central question, the one question that can arouse not only the Fisher King but the whole Cosmos: Where is the supreme reality, the sacred, the Centre of Life and the source of immortality, where is the Holy Graal? ...

That brief episode of a great European myth reveals to us at least one neglected aspect of the symbolism of the Centre: that there is not only an intimate interconnection between the universal life and the salvation of man; but that *it is enough only to raise the question of salvation*, to pose the central problem; that is, *the* problem – for the life of the cosmos to be for ever renewed. For – as this mythological fragment seems to show – death is only the result of our indifference to immortality.[17]

A SPECTRUM OF HYPOTHESES

1) When he becomes aware of the existence of many religions, the conscious man feels that in order to be sure of the truth of the one he has chosen, he has to study and compare all of them and then decide. Because his logic seems to demand that he adhere to the religion proven to be the best, he asks himself: "How can I pinpoint and recognize the value of each and every construction?" Even here, the official attitude of modern, contemporary rationalism betrays its abstract nature: it is only by knowing all religions that an individual can choose, in conscience, what appears to be the most appropriate and truthful. This is not an ideal but rather a utopia. It implies a task that is, in fact, in practice unrealizable. Mircea Eliade's testimony is interesting even if only from the perspective of a historian of religions:

What nobler or more rewarding occupation could there be than to frequent the great mystics of all the religions, to live among symbols and mysteries, to read and understand the myths of all the nations? The layman imagines that a historian of religions must be equally at home with the Greek or the Egyptian mythology, with the authentic teaching of the Buddha, the Taoist mysteries or the secret rites of initiation in archaic society ... Yet in fact the situation is quite different. A good many historians of religions are so absorbed in their special studies that they know little more about the Greek or Egyptian mythologies, or the Buddha's teaching, or the Taoist or shamanic techniques, than any amateur who has known how to direct his reading. Most of them are really familiar with only one poor little sector of the immense domain of religious history ... We wanted at all costs to present an *objective* history of religions, but we failed to bear in mind that what we were christening *objectivity* followed the fashion of thinking in our times."[18]

Hoping to know all religions in order to choose the best is utopian and whatever is utopian is a false ideal. The ideal is the dynamism of man's nature in motion and, at every step along the way, something of the ideal is fulfilled. Utopia is foreign to nature. It is a superimposed dream, often a pretext for escaping reality or forcing its hand. Utopia always means violence. The assumption that we must know all religions produced by the history of man in order to make a rationally dignified choice is an abstract criterion, impossible to apply. And, in the final analysis, a criterion ceases to be natural and reasonable when it cannot be applied.

2) We could fall back, then, on the principle of at least striving to know the major religions, for example, those with the largest following, like Christianity, Islam, and Buddhism. But how could this criterion have been applied 2,000 years ago in Rome, when Tacitus and Svetonius were writing that a handful of people lived in the city whom they believed were a "small sect" of Jews connected with "someone called Christ"? They were Christians and, if I had been living in that time and place, if I had followed the suggestion of learned opinion, I would have had to ignore that tiny group of men, and I would never have discovered that it was there that the truth of my person lay. If a criterion is true, it should be able to be applied in all cases.

3) One final illustration of enlightenment abstractedness is the syncretic notion. This idea creates a type of universal religion which progressively takes the best from all religions, so it is always iridescent, a synthesis of the best of humanity. But this does not consider that what might be the best for one man, might not be the best for others. Here we find the typical presumption of a society whereby people must prostrate themselves before the will of a group of "enlightened" ones. If my religious temperament leads me to discover A, and if another person arrives at B, and a third wishes to create C comprising the best of A and B, C would still not have the required features of

something universal because it would still constitute a choice as idiosyncratic as A and B.

4) The empirical solution seems instead to be more correct. Man is born into a certain environment, at a particular moment in history, and it is highly probable that the religion his surroundings profess will be the expression best suited to his temperament. Thus, if we really want to lay down a law, which although not absolute is convenient, we should conclude that every man should follow the religion of his own tradition. Perhaps an encounter in life will draw attention to a doctrine, a morality, an emotion more suited to our reason matured over time or to our heart with its particular history. In that case, we could well "change," "convert" (Cardinal John Henry Newman noted that "conversion" is nothing other than the deeper, more authentic discovery of what we have always adhered to). But the suggestion that we follow the religion of our own tradition remains a basic unpretentious directive. In this sense then, all religions are "true." Man's only duty is to be serious in adhering to them.

2 The Need for Revelation

When faced with his destiny, with his ultimate meaning, man imagines its ways, which are the projection of his resources. But the more serious his reflection and emotions, the more he suffers from the ultimate enigma, like a storm of uncertainty, or the loneliness of bewilderment. Only the divine itself can adequately help the man who recognizes his existential impotence, that hidden divinity, the mystery which somehow becomes involved with man's trials, enlightening and sustaining him along his pathway.

This cannot be anything but a perfectly reasonable hypothesis, that is, corresponding to the impetus and coherent with the openness of human nature, fully inscribed within the great category of possibility. Reason cannot define what the mystery can or cannot do. In order to remain faithful to itself, it cannot exclude any initiative the mystery might undertake. If reason presumed to impose a measure on the divine, for example, to admit the possibility that the divine could join the human game and sustain man along his pathway – if it were to go so far as to deny revelation, it would be the "ultimate and extreme form of idolatry, the extreme attempt that reason makes to impose on God its own image of him."[1] Above all other considerations, this would be a supreme act of irrationality. At the heart of the greatest artistic expressions in all places and eras is the presentiment or the affirmation of the hypothesis that the divine can help man. From Plato to Leopardi, reason cries out for it and launches itself towards this hypothesis, which is so rational and so much a part of our nature that, to some degree, it always emerges.

Let us examine some instances illustrating how this need for revelation and the claim to fulfil it have been articulated in the religious history of humanity. Underlying the need for revelation is man's expectation of an adequate response from that meaning of life which he can neither pin down as theoretical knowledge nor acquire by a contest of strength. We will now run through a brief list of the testimonies of some great scholars with the sole aim of documenting to what degree man's need for the mystery to reply to the ultimate human question is experienced as a manifestation of the mystery itself, a way in which it becomes present on man's weary road.

a) The first observation regards knowledge. Throughout his history, man has always expressed the conviction that his own enlightenment regarding what is "Totally Other," the Unknown, is possible since it is precisely the Unknown which desires to be manifest in reality. "Man knows the sacred because the sacred makes itself manifest. An hierophany is a manifestation of the sacred, a mysterious act by which what is 'totally distinct' from us manifests itself in an object or in a being of this profane world. All types of hierophanies constitute a complex religious phenomenon incorporating the being or the natural object and what is 'totally distinct,' made manifest through the being or object. In manifesting itself, it confers on this being or object a sacred dimension which permits it to fulfil a mediation role."[2]

Man has multiplied the ideal places for these manifestations. As Mircea Eliade says:

Every microcosm, every inhabited region has what may be called a 'Center'; that is to say, a place that is sacred above all. It is there, in that center, that the sacred manifests itself in its totality ... But we must not envisage this symbolism of the Center with the geometrical implications that it has to the western scientific mind. For each one of these microcosms there may be several "centers" ... All the Oriental civilizations – Mesopotamia, India, China, etc. – recognize an unlimited number of "Centers" ... What we have here is a sacred, mythic geography, the only kind effectually real, as opposed to profane geography, the latter being "objective" and, as it were, abstract and non-essential – the theoretical construction of a space and a world we do not live in, and therefore do not *know*.[3]

The great Romanian historian of religions goes on to show us how symbol and myth played their part in the history of man as the instruments par excellence for knowledge and revelation of the mystery, the means for overcoming the ephemeral and being immersed in the permanent. "In the archaic world the myth alone is real. It tells of manifestations of the only indubitable reality – the *sacred*."[4] "[T]he narration of the myths is not without consequences for him who recites and those who listen. From the mere fact of the narration of a myth, profane time is – at least symbolically – abolished: the narrator and his hearers are rapt into sacred and mythical time ... the myth implies a breakaway from Time and the surrounding world; it opens up a way into the sacred Great Time."[5]

Julien Ries's definition of myth becomes clear at this point when he comments on Eliade's scientific contribution to the question: "A myth is a story which is true, sacred and exemplary, which has a specific meaning and which entails repetition, which gives rise to a tradition ... Myths serve to awaken and sustain awareness of a different world from the profane, the divine world."[6] And Eliade's eloquent passage is also clear: "In other words, one goes beyond the temporal condition and the dull self-sufficiency which is the lot of every human being simply because every human being is 'ignorant' – in the sense that he is identifying himself, and Reality, with his own particular situation. And ignorance is, first of all, this false identification of Reality with what each one of us *appears to be or to possess*. A politician thinks that the one true reality is political power, a millionaire is convinced that wealth alone is real, a man of learning thinks the same conviction about his studies, his books, laboratories and so forth."[7]

One of the most noble of human efforts is the attempt to go beyond appearances and contingent circumstances and to strive to grasp the most incorruptible, original, and mysterious aspects of life. "Religious symbolism, in the existence and life of the *homo religiosus*, serves for revelation. Through symbols, the world speaks and reveals forms of the real that in themselves are not visible. The symbol is the language of hierophany since it allows us to make contact with the sacred. Religious symbols which touch life's structures reveal a life that transcends the natural, human dimension."[8]

b) The second observation, implicit in the first, concerns the fact that man has always recognized – in addition to the cosmic and natural realities as pathways to the divine – his constant need for other men to be mediators. Referring to the significance and importance of shamanism in the religions of ancient Eurasia, Eliade comments: "There exist 'specialists of the sacred,' men capable of 'seeing' the spirits, of climbing to Heaven and meeting the gods, of descending to Hell and combatting demons, illnesses and death."[9] A noteworthy example is an ancient form of Chinese shamanism, wuism. The Wu were characterized by their power to make "close personal contact with divinities and spirits."[10] In one moving poetic passage describing a meeting with the divinity, the Wu woman proclaims:

> With great bounds my god descends. Oh, there he is!
> All light and splendour, so clear and limitless!

Then, after the hospitality rite, the god leaves and the woman watches him go with this verse of regret:

> But great is the desire for god, deep is my sigh
> Contrite is my heart, heaving with sadness.[11]

In awaiting revelation, there is an underlying anxiety, something disturbing, born of the intuition that a lost relationship will be recovered by the ensuing encounter. "Throughout Chinese history we find what could be called the nostalgia for paradise, that is, the desire to reenact, through ecstasy, a 'primordial situation': the situation represented by the original unity/totality (hun-tun), or the time when human beings could meet the gods directly."[12] Here we have the "obsession with what is real, the primitive man's thirst for being."[13]

Naturally, human history has recorded many other versions of this specialization in the sacred, or rather, the trust men have placed in other men to conduct their relationship with the divine. One aspect of this phenomenon is more strictly political. Tibet provides us with the following example: "In the traditional religion, the role of the king was fundamental. The sovereign's divine nature manifested itself in his 'splendor' and in his magical powers. The first kings remained on earth only by day; at night they returned to Heaven. They did not die in the ordinary sense, but at a certain moment made their definitive reascent to Heaven on their magic rope, mu (or dmu) ... [which in] Tibetan religious thought ... filled a cosmological function: it joined Earth and Heaven like an axis mundi ... "[14]

c) In the context of the religions of ancient Greece, which, as we have seen, remained far removed from any hope of a relationship with the divine, the Dionysian experience signifies the profound and somewhat perturbing human desire for revelation.

More than the other Greek gods, Dionysus astonishes by the multiplicity and novelty of his epiphanies, by the variety of his transformations. He is always in motion; he makes his way everywhere, into all countries, among all peoples, into every religious milieu, ready to associate himself with various divinities (even with such antagonistic deities as Demeter and Apollo). He is certainly the only Greek god who, revealing himself under different aspects, dazzles and attracts both peasants and the intellectual elite, politicians and contemplatives, orgiastics and ascetics. Intoxication, eroticism, universal fertility, but also the unforgettable experiences inspired by the periodic arrival of the dead, or by *mania*, by immersion in animal unconsciousness, or by the ecstasy of *enthousiasmos* – all these terrors and revelations spring from a single source: *the presence of the god*. His mode of being expresses the paradoxical unity of life and death. This is why Dionysus constitutes a type of divinity radically different from the Olympians. Was he *nearer* to human beings than the other gods? In any case, one could approach him, could even incorporate him; and the ecstasy of *mania* proved that the human condition could be surpassed.[15]

It is also true, of course, that at the time of Imperial Rome – "an age terrorized by the omnipotence of Destiny" – in the texts of popular hermeticism testimonies resound with the belief that the presence of a god would satisfy man's innermost thirst for knowledge and dominion over nature in order to have a better life: "Since it is a matter of discovering a whole network of sympathies and antipathies that nature maintains secretly, how can this secret be penetrated unless a god reveals it?"[16]

   d) All founders of religions have in common the certainty that they are the bearers of an essential revelation of their God. In his reference to the Iranian religion, for example, Eliade comments: "Zarathustra declares that he 'recognized' Ahura Mazda 'by thought alone,' 'as the first and last' (Y. 31:8) – as the beginning and the end." He "receives the revelation of the new religion directly from Ahura Mazda. By accepting it, he imitates the primordial act of the Lord – the choice of Good (see Yasna 32:2), and he asks nothing else of his disciples."[17] Eliade continues:

We are struck, furthermore, by the urgency and existential tension with which Zarathustra questions his Lord: he asks him to teach him the secrets of the cosmogony, to reveal his future to him, but also the fate of certain persecutors and of all the wicked. Each Strophe of the celebrated *Yasna* 44 is introduced by the same formula: "This is what I ask you, Lord – answer me well!" Zarathustra wants to know "who assigned their road to the sun and the stars" (3), "who fixed the earth below, and the sky of clouds, so that it does not fall" (4); and his questions concerning the Creation follow one another in an ever faster rhythm. But he wants to know, too, how his soul, "arrived at the Good, will be ravished?" (8), and "how shall we get rid of evil" (13).[18]

Eternal questions, whose rhythm will be ever-present until the end of time. Man has always awaited an answer to these questions from the mysterious Origin of all things.

The ambiance of the Koran texts is different, yet, in the same way as those we have cited, affirm that revelation is given to a man chosen by God, which enables him and humanity to know him better and to live in a more adequate way with respect to human dignity. The Koran describes the ways revelation appears: "God can speak to no man except by Revelation, or from behind a veil, or else he sends a Messenger who, with His permission, reveals what He wants to man." The historical work, at-Tabari, contains a description of divine illumination: " ... At the beginning of Revelation there came to the God-sent the one true vision ... ; it came (upon him) like dawn's breaking."[19]

God deploys diverse circumstances and images to reveal himself to his chosen.

As if impelled by a presentiment, Muhammad returned to Mecca in February/March 632; this was his last pilgrimage ... And the Angel dictated to him these words of Allah: "Today I have perfected your religion for you, and I completed My blessing upon you, and I have approved Islam for your religion" (5:5–6). According to the tradition, at the end of his "Pilgrimage of Farewell," Muhammad cried out: "Lord! Have I fulfilled my mission well?" And the crowd replied: "Yes, you have fulfilled it well!" ... Another tradition supplies a stairway which Muhammad climbs, led on by the angel Gabriel, to the gates of Heaven. He arrives before Allah and learns from his mouth that he has been chosen before all the other prophets and that he, Muhammad, is his "friend."[20]

The founder of Manichaeism, Mani, also was certain that he had established a great universal religion based on revelations he received at the age of twelve and twenty-four when "an angel brought him messages from the 'King of the Paradise of lights' (the supreme and good God of Manichaeism) ... ." He was given the following assurance: "As a river joins another river to form a strong current, so the old books are added together in my Scriptures; and they have formed a great Wisdom, such as has not existed in previous generations."[21] However, Mani is aware that he has created something given to him from above. This is how he expresses himself in a stormy exchange with his king: "When Mani proclaimed the divine character of his mission, Bahram burst out: 'Why was this revelation made to thee, and not to Us, who are the masters of the land?' Mani could answer only 'Such is the will of God.' "[22]

Eliade's comments on the Manichaean revelation are interesting. "The Manichaean theology, cosmogony, and anthropogony seem to answer any and every question concerning 'origins.' It is understandable why the Manichaeans regarded their doctrine as more true, that is, more 'scientific,' than the other religions: it is because it explained the totality of the real by a chain of causes and their effects. In truth, there is a certain likeness between Manichaeism and scientific materialism, both ancient and modern: for the one as for the other, the world, life, and man are the result of a chance happening."[23]

This is the consequence of the anxiousness of man. He searches for solutions and answers within the Enigma, and in his preoccupation forgets the questions!

e) Lastly, because it is more familiar to the Christian West of today, we shall consider the certainty of revelation in the faith of Israel.

The faith of Israel does not present itself as a proclamation of the purest transcendence of God by means of a series of abstract theological theorems. But in contrast to the indigenous Canaanite religion, neither does it presume to be an immanentist celebration of the divinity reduced to the level of the biological mechanisms of sexual fertility and seasonal rhythms. The "creed" of Israel, documented in Deut. 26:4–9; Josh. 24:1–13; Ps. 136, chooses history and time as the privileged setting for God to make himself manifest. So he remains transcendent but entrusts his presence and his words to the reality most inherent in man – history. This is the meaning of the celebrated oracle of Nathan recorded in 2 Sam. 7 and in Ps. 89: David's desire to offer God a holy place (bayit, "house") which would enclose the sacred meets the opposition of Yahweh who wants the gift of his presence to be held within the "house" – bayit of David's dynasty, within history itself.[24]

This concept of a God who reveals himself in history implies the intuition that continuity in the relationship between man and God is possible; "the event" becomes a concrete starting point for this relationship, a stimulus, a teaching. "The faith of Israel is invariably related to an event, a divine self-declaration in history."[25] This continuity is the drawstring binding together events in the life of an entire people. "We see this people perennially driven, moved, formed, transformed, annihilated and re-born through the word of God that is always pronounced anew."[26] We might share the view of one Old Testament scholar who said: "In summary, Yahweh and man have a continuous relationship but this relationship is prior to revelation itself and preparatory to it: it appears to be the condition for the perfect encounter."[27]

FACING AN UNIMAGINABLE CLAIM

In the previous chapter, we have seen that all religions are true in the nobility of the rational, moral, and aesthetic effort they express, and that man, driven by the needs of his humanity, must make this effort and therefore have a religion. We have just observed that the need for revelation is at the root of this attempt, and this is true of the most diverse religious experiences.

Within the freedom and variety of attempts that are made and messages conveyed, a religion may commit only one crime : to say "I am the religion, the one and only way." And this is precisely what Christianity claims. This constitutes a crime, the moral imposition of its own expression on others. So there is nothing wrong in feeling repelled by such an affirmation: what would be wrong would be to leave unquestioned such an affirmation, the reason for this great claim.

3 The Enigma as a Fact Within the Human Trajectory

Man's demand for revelation sums up the condition of his spirit in conceiving of and realizing the relationship with the divine according to the alternative that this diagram expresses.

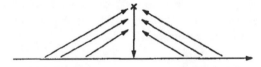

The horizontal line represents the trajectory of human history, above which looms the presence of an x: destiny, fate, the ultimate something, mystery, "God."

Throughout the trajectory of history, in theoretical and practical terms, humanity has sought to comprehend the relationship binding its contingent reality, its ephemeral point, and its ultimate meaning, to imagine and live the link between its own transitory nature and the eternal. Let us suppose that the enigma of x, the enigmatic presence looming beyond the horizon (without which reason could not be reason, because reason is the affirmation of the ultimate meaning) were to penetrate the fabric of history, join in the flow of time and space and, with an unimaginable expressive force, become a "Fact" incarnate in our midst. But, in this hypothesis, what does "incarnate" mean? It means to assume that this mysterious x became a phenomenon, a regular fact that could act upon and be registered in the trajectory of history.

This supposition would correspond to the need for revelation. It would be irrational to exclude the possibility that the mystery, which makes all things, could reach the point where it becomes directly and personally involved with man in the trajectory of history. For we have already seen how, by our very nature, we cannot prescribe the boundaries of mystery. Therefore, given the possibility of the fact and the rationality of the hypothesis, what is left for us to do when confronted with it? We can only ask ourselves: *did it or did it not happen?*

If it did happen, this would be the only path to follow, not because the others are false, but because God would have charted it. The mystery would have presented itself as a historical fact from which no one who had seriously and sincerely faced it could dissociate himself without denying his own path. By accepting and travelling this pathway traced by God, man would become aware that this road, when compared with others, proves to be a more human synthesis, a more complete way of valuing the factors at play. In following that exceptional pathway, I should, as a matter of course, acquire a better understanding of the other roads as I gradually become acquainted with them, and, in the process, obtain the capacity to perceive the good within them. This would be a broad and richly magnanimous experience, which appreciates the true value of these other pathways. It would be an experience able to embrace all values, "catholic" in the etymological sense of the word – all-encompassing, universal. A Second Vatican Council document advises:

The Catholic Church does not reject anything that is true and holy in these religions. It is sincerely respectful of these ways of acting and living and of these rules and doctrines, and although they may differ on many points from what the Church believes and proposes, they often bring a ray of the truth which enlightens all men ... The Church therefore exhorts its sons so that with caution and charity, through dialogue and collaboration with those who adhere to other religions, and by continuing to bear witness to the Christian faith and life, they will recognize, preserve and allow the advancement of the spiritual, moral and socio-cultural values found in them.[1]

Within this hypothesis proposing that the mystery looming beyond man's horizon crossed the line of the arcane and penetrated man's pathway, we are faced with a radical change between this "religious" form and every other human attempt to forge a relationship with the unknown. But seriously considering this hypothesis as true does not diminish attentive, congenial openness towards all other human research.

A RADICAL OVERTURNING OF THE
RELIGIOUS METHOD

The hypothesis that the mystery has penetrated man's existence by speaking to him in human terms alters the man-destiny relationship which will no longer be based on human effort, the fruit of man's construction or imagination, the study of a distant, enigmatic thing, or on waiting for something absent. Instead, it will mean coming up against something present. If God had manifested a particular will in a particular way in human history, if he had charted a pathway of his own leading us to him, the central issue of the religious phenomenon would cease to be man attempting to imagine God, even though this attempt is the greatest expression of human dignity; instead, the whole issue would lie in freedom's pure and simple gesture of acceptance or rejection. This is the overturning of the method. No longer is the focal point the striving of the intelligence, the drive of the will to construct, the stretching of the imagination, the weaving of a complex moralism. Rather, it is simple recognition, the reaction of one who, watching out for the arrival of a friend, singles him out of the crowd and greets him. In this hypothesis, the religious method would lose all of its disturbing connotations of an enigmatic deferment to something in the distance. Rather, it would have the dynamics of an experience, the experience of a present, an encounter.

It should be noted that the first method favours the intelligent man, the cultured, the fortunate, the powerful, while the second favours the poor, the ordinary man. To encounter a person who is present is as easy for a child to grasp as an adult. In this hypothesis, the dynamics of revelation would cease to primarily emphasize ingeniousness and initiative, but would stress simplicity and love. Love, in fact, represents man's only true dependence, the affirmation of the Other as our very substance, the supreme choice of freedom. But under such an hypothesis, it would no longer be presumptuous to affirm only one pathway. It would be obedience to a fact, the decisive Fact of all time.

One way to escape remains – to deny that this Fact is possible at all. Such a crime against the supreme category of reason, of possibility, was condemned by Graham Greene's priest in the face of the crazed hate of a "free thinker." In *The End of the Affair*, the priest demonstrated hatred's profound contradiction by saying that it seemed more like free thinking to admit all possibilities rather than to preclude some of them.[2]

NO LONGER JUST AN HYPOTHESIS

We have seen that this hypothesis is possible and, if true, would revolutionize the religious method. We must now recognize that it was and is believed to be true in the history of man. The Christian message says: "Yes, this happened."

Let us picture the world as an immense plain where numerous groups of human beings, under the direction of engineers and architects, are busy working on disparate projects to build bridges with thousands of arches serving as links between earth and heaven, between the ephemeral place of their existence and the "star" of destiny. With its infinite number of building sites, the plain is a hive of activity. At a certain point a man arrives on the scene, and his gaze embraces the whole frenzied workplace. Suddenly he shouts: "Stop!" Those closest to him cease working, and then gradually the others follow until they are all watching him. And he tells them: "You are great and noble. You are making a sublime effort, but it is an unhappy one because you will never manage to build a road linking your world with the ultimate mystery. Abandon your projects, lay down your tools. Destiny has taken pity on you. Follow me and I will build the bridge, for *I* am destiny." Now let us try to imagine the reaction of all of those people to such a declaration. First the architects, then the work foremen, then the best of the artisans would find themselves telling their labourers instinctively: "Don't stop working. Keep going. Can't you see this man is crazy?" And they would echo: "Of course, he must be crazy." Resuming their work on their bosses' orders, others might say: "You can see he's crazy." There would be just a few who would not take their eyes off this man, for they have been profoundly moved. They would not obey their bosses as the masses had done, but would approach and follow him.

Within this flight of fancy is the story of what happened in history and is still happening now.

At this point, we no longer find ourselves confronting a theoretical (philosophical or moral) problem, but an historical one. The first question we must ask is not: "Is what the Christian message says reasonable or right?" but "Did it happen or not?" or "Did God really intervene in history?"

Although implied in our earlier discussion, I would like to stress that this "new" question requires a different method, which could be explained like this: man may, indeed must, arrive at the discovery of the existence of a mysterious something, of God, through his analytical perception of his own experience of reality (and we have seen how ample historical documentation demonstrates that man normally reaches this discovery in this way); the issue now, since it is a question of an historical fact, cannot be verified by analytical reflection on the structure of one's own relationship with reality. It is a fact that either happened in history or did not: it either exists or does not, it either transpired or did not. It was either a real event which emerged in man's existence as part of history and therefore must be recognized as an event, or it remains just a notion. Faced with this hypothesis, the method is the historical registration of an objective fact.

Then, the question: "Did God really intervene in history?" must refer, above all, to that incomparable claim which is the content of a precise message. It must necessarily become another question: "Who is Jesus?" Christianity arises as the answer to this question.

A PROBLEM THAT MUST BE SOLVED

In *The Brothers Karamazov*, Fyodor Dostoyevsky writes: "faith is reduced to this anguished problem: can an educated man, a contemporary European believe, really believe in the divinity of the son of God, Jesus Christ?"[3] By now the religious problem plays itself out at the level of this question. In any case and for any individual who hears it, the mere fact that even one man claims: "God was made man," presents a radical, unavoidable problem for the religious life of humanity.

Sören Kierkegaard wrote in his *Journals*: "The basest form of scandal in human terms is to leave the whole problem of Christ without a solution. The truth is that the Christian imperative – you must – has been completely forgotten. That Christianity has been announced to you means that *you must* assume a position in Christ's regard. He himself, or the fact that He exists, or the fact that He existed represents the one decision to be made in life."[4] There are certain provocations that, because of their radical nature, man cannot eliminate or censure once he has perceived them, if he is to act as a man. Man is forced to answer yes or no. The mere fact that he has heard the news that one man declared: "I am God," means that he cannot be indifferent to it. He must arrive at his own conviction as to whether the news is true or false. A man cannot passively allow himself to be diverted or distracted from such a problem, and it is in this sense that Kierkegaard uses the word "scandal" in keeping with its authentic Greek origins where "skándalon" means impediment, hindrance. The man who immediately or gradually allows himself to be distracted from the possibility of forming a personal opinion about the problem of Christ is hindering himself from being a man. As a side note, I would point out that we can be convinced that we live like Christians, inserted in what I would call the "Christian ranks," without having resolved this problem for ourselves, without having freed ourselves from that impediment.

A fact has its own inevitability. Depending upon the importance of its content, eluding a fact in the persistent, irrational distracted way which man, paradoxically, is capable of, seriously deforms the human personality. If we were driving a truck along a two-metre wide road and suddenly found that a landslide was blocking the road, we could not proceed, we would have to resolve the situation. We would then find ourselves faced with what Kierkegaard calls in the above passage a "must," an imperative, a problem that must be resolved.

The Christian imperative is that the content of its message presents itself as a fact. This cannot be stressed enough. An insidious cultural disloyalty, aided by the ambiguity and fragility of Christians as well, has facilitated the dissemination of a vague notion of Christianity as a discourse or doctrine and perhaps, therefore, a fable or moral. No. First and foremost it is a fact – a man joined the ranks of men.

But the imperative embraces another aspect of the fact: the advent of that man is an announcement transmitted down through the years to us today. To this very day, this event has been proclaimed and announced as the event of a Presence. That one man said: "I am God," and that this is passed on as a present fact, forcefully demands a personal stance. We can smile about it or decide not to bother with it: this would mean, in any case, that we decided to resolve the problem in a negative way, that we have not wanted to face up to a proposal whose dimensions are so great that they are beyond the realms of human imagination.

This is why society so often turns away from this announcement and wishes to confine it to churches and the individual conscience. What society finds most disturbing is the vastness of the dimensions of the problem: whether he did or did not exist, or rather, whether *he does exist* or *existed*; whether we can verify it or not; this is the greatest decision of our existence. No other choice that society could propose or man could imagine as important has this value. And it sounds like an imposition. The affirmation of the Christian message appears to be despotism. But is announcing the news of something that happened, however great, really despotism?

A PROBLEM OF FACT

We must be aware that the problem concerns a question of fact. From reason's point of view, it is a source of bitterness that we date all events from the birth of Christ, and yet so few have bothered to ask about the problem of Christ historically speaking. This is neither a problem of opinions or tastes, nor one of analyzing the religious soul

– an exploration of the religious sense does not tell us whether Christianity communicates a true or false announcement. I have already outlined this position in the first volume[5] of this trilogy: the method is imposed by the object, not the subject. And since the religious sense is a phenomenon of the person, the method to approach it – and this should be faced again and again – is self-reflection. That Christ did or did not say he was God, whether he is God or not, and the fact that he is still reaching us even today, is an historical issue. The method, therefore, must correspond to it and be as serious as the problem itself.

I would like to digress briefly at this point. Sometimes certain expressions such as these can be heard: "The Christians have Christ, just as the Buddhists have Buddha or the Moslems Mohammed." Although it is obvious that such affirmations are born of ignorance, we must be made aware of this, however summarily.

The Christian message is this: a man who ate, walked, and lived the normal life of a man proclaimed: "I am your destiny," "I am he of whom the whole Cosmos is made." Objectively, this is the only case in history where a man did not declare himself divine in a generic way, but substantially identified himself with God. From the viewpoint of the history of humanity's religious sentiment, it must be noted that the greater man's religious genius, the more he perceives and experiences his distance from God, the supremacy of God, the disproportion between God and the human being. The religious experience is precisely the lived awareness of the smallness of man, of the incommensurability of the mystery. We are told that when St Francis was found in the Verna woods lying face down in the undergrowth, he was repeating: "Who are you? Who am I?" In this way, he fixed the abyss of difference between man and God, the two poles, which create the fascination of religious sentiment. The deeper this sentiment, the more it is like lightning shooting forth – powerful, bright, and burning – and the more man feels the potential difference between these two poles. Just as the more religious genius a man possesses, the less he feels tempted to identify himself with the divine. Man can certainly act, "pretending" to be God, but it is theoretically impossible to conceive of identifying himself with God. Structurally, man cannot identify his evident incompleteness with the whole, except by betraying a flagrantly pathological condition. The normal dynamism of the intelligence is prevented from falling into this temptation because to exist at all, every temptation must arise from a likelihood, a shadow of possibility. And for man to really conceive of himself as God is unlikely, without a semblance of possibility.

4 How the Problem Arose in History

There is a fact of history that claims to be the very realization of the hypothesis that the mystery penetrated the trajectory of history as an inherent and therefore earthly, human factor. We have seen that the further removed religious genius is from this claim, the more authentic it is. We now find ourselves faced with a religious phenomenon which instead is based on this very claim. Let us first reflect on the information that has been transmitted to us in the form of recorded data, and then we will explore the content of the claim.

THE FACT AS CRITERION

We have inherited an historical document that shows us how the problem arose originally: the Gospels. The nature of this document has posed a few problems for historical enquiry. Before examining this record of the facts as they have been handed down to us, let us make a few observations.

a) We should initially clarify what the Gospels are *not*. We will thus avoid using a method inadequate for the object at hand since, as has been shown, we cannot know an object except by the method it expressly requires.

We could borrow some examples of these negative definitions of the Gospels from various authors – there are so many that we only have to choose. This one is well known: "The evangelists ... had no intention of providing a shorthand record of what Christ said or a report of his actions such as a police officer might do."[1] The author continues in the same way in his introduction to his text on the Gospel of John: "[Jesus'] discourses in John cannot and do not intend to be historical reporting or a word for word record."[2] This is how the council document *Dei Verbum* describes the activity of the evangelists:

After the ascension of the Lord, by virtue of that most total of wisdoms taught them by the glorious events of Christ and enlightened by the Spirit of truth, the apostles passed on to their listeners all that he had said and done. And the sacred authors wrote the four Gospels, choosing some aspects among the many which were relayed verbally or in written form. They summarized some, explained others according to the various churches' situations and conserved the message's nature of an announcement but always in such a way that their references to Jesus himself were made in sincerity and truth.[3]

And Walter Kasper comments: "There are three distinct degrees in the tradition of the Gospels – what Jesus himself said and did; what the apostles after Easter and in the light of the resurrection and the advent of the Spirit 'transmitted ... with that most total of wisdoms they ... enjoyed'; finally, the evangelists' editing of the Gospels by which, according to the various churches' situations, they selected some aspects, summarized others, explained still others and con- served throughout their sermon-like nature."[4]

We are thus advised that we are not presented with all of the facts as they happened but with some that, nevertheless, did happen and which have come down to us from the memories of witnesses, spurred by the urgency and the imperative of relaying their import- ance to individuals and all humanity. For example, if a new car I had long desired and bought after much sacrifice was stolen and then turned up again, I could come to know about this in two ways. First, I might be summoned to the police station to read a report indicating that in a given street they had found an abandoned car with no tires or registration plate, but whose description fitted my own report of the theft. Or secondly, I might receive an excited telephone call from a friend telling me that from the bus he has seen my car in a side street. He cannot remember which street exactly, but he is sure he could find it again. He does not go into detail about the car he saw but assures me it is mine. Then I would go to see it for myself. I have, therefore, heard the news in two reasonably reliable ways. Only the methods of verification differ.

 b) We find ourselves, therefore, with a document, which, like others, is based upon *memory* and, in an original way, intends to make an *announcement*. The form of the document reflects its intention. Its historical value can be grasped as long as this characteristic is not disregarded: it seeks to trace the memory of an exceptional fact which someone, believing it was vital to tell others, transmitted. "But these traditions concern Jesus as well as the resurrected Christ. This does not necessarily lessen their documentary value, for the essential element of Christianity – as is also the case with any religion laying claim to a founder – is precisely *memory*. It is the *memory of Jesus* that constitutes the model for every Christian. But the tradition handed down by the earliest witnesses was 'exemplary,' not simply 'historical'; it preserved the significant structures of events and the preaching, not any precise recollection of Jesus's activity. The phenomenon is well known, and not only in the history of religions."[5]

Now that we have confirmed that we are not dealing with a shorthand record, a word-for-word account, or a draft of a news report, we must confront the object as it appears – as a memory and an announcement – in order to understand it. We must face it in its totality and ask ourselves: "Is it plausible? Is it convincing?" Any other method would evade the object as it is today and would, therefore, be applied to something, that was, in the final analysis, non-existent.

The full futility becomes apparent of the efforts of those exegetes – whether they are believers or not – who strive to achieve something like a "neutral" photograph and tape-recording of the historical Jesus. Taking photographs is a physical event, and the equipment can by its nature capture nothing other than what is offered to it physically, even if this is the features of a human face. The writing of history, on the other hand, asks questions about meaning, and essentially it cannot obtain any more meaning than it itself is ready to deposit and invest in anticipation. What historiography is prepared to give in this case is revealed by the different clichés of its respective portraits of Jesus. These portraits mostly brush over what is precisely the essential feature: the claim of Jesus that runs through all his words and deeds and which is a challenge to Jesus-historians to be less stingy with the range of meaning they allow the text.[6]

The claim Jesus makes is precisely the one fact with which it is interesting to come into contact. It is the only compelling fact for the intelligence of man and requires, as an imperative, a solution. One, therefore, should not risk overlooking it, but must place himself advantageously in order to attain a conviction about it (cf p. 33). Now, a conviction is always based upon something which is "demonstrated." But, as explained elsewhere,[7] for the most important things in our lives, this demonstrability is never mathematical or dialectical, as in the case of a creation or a postulation of our own. Rather, the type of demonstration we are discussing is given by the evident encounter with a fact, coming to grips with an event.

We must remember that we cannot come to grips with the event if we are not ready to be provoked by its totality. This is what H.U. von Balthasar called "being less stingy with the ... meaning." The inevitable price to pay for being "stingy" is that we lose sight of the whole point – we try to evade the totality of the fact by seeking only some aspects of it or allowing ourselves to be convinced by one type of element as opposed to another. The very force of this unheard-of claim is what makes the search interesting and can only be sought in the entirety of the fact. The following observations of von Balthasar seem very persuasive to me:

The first prerequisite for understanding is to accept what is given just as it offers itself. If certain excisions are practised on the Gospel from the outset, the integrity of the phenomenon is lost and it has already become incomprehensible ... Not the smallest plausible interconnection is then retained, because each element is plausible only within the wholeness of the image ... If nonetheless essential portions are excluded, what is left is such a paltry construction (such as Renan's historical Jesus, or Harnack's or even Bultmann's) that its academic provenance may be detected at a distance, and then one is still left with the problem of explaining how so slight a kernel could become such a full-powered and seamless form as is the Christ of the Gospels. In this resulting form, it might be possible to try to explain certain inconsistencies by philological enquiry, by distinguishing different sources and layers, the different character of the documents, and so on. But even then one has not accounted for – or rather, has not seen or recognized – that tension-laden and supremely plausible total form that is yielded when all these aspects are taken together.[8]

We must, therefore, be willing to let ourselves be provoked by the entire fact which is more than the sum of its factors. The council document we have already mentioned reiterates this, and in his comment on it, Henri de Lubac reminds us:

Now, for the Council as well, the object of Revelation is God himself; but this living God intervened in the history of men and He gave us witnesses in history and these witnesses refer us to the one supreme Witness, to that true and faithful Witness who is His word made flesh. The first object of my faith does not consist in a list of *truths* that are intelligible or not ... If this object is *incomprehensible* to me in the etymological sense – and how could I ever wish that that were so? – if I cannot circumscribe it as I would if it were a creation of my own spirit, this is because it is ... the embrace of a living Person ... This is the essential factor: the object revealed is not conceived as a series of propositions ... but recognized in its original unity as the mystery of Christ, the reality of a personal, living being.[9]

The story we are about to approach aims to trace the course of an encounter with the bearer and object of the most extraordinary revealing claim ever made in the history of man. Again de Lubac warns: "It is impossible to dissociate Him from his Gospel ... periodically, men have tried: but it is like seeking to divide the indivisible. It is a betrayal of the one Gospel, which is, as the opening lines of St. Mark say, *the good news about Jesus Christ, the Son of God* (Mark 1:1). Fr. Pierre Rousselot (1915) put it admirably when he wrote over fifty years ago: 'Christianity is based on a fact, the fact of Jesus, the earthly life of Jesus. Even today, Christians are those people who believe that Jesus still lives. This is the fundamental originality of the Christian religion.' "[10]

A fact is a criterion that everyone can grasp. We can encounter a fact, come face to face with it, providing we have placed ourselves favourably in order to see it. How, then, can we grasp the fact of Christ so that we can go on to evaluate its claim? We can begin by retracing the memory of him, and the announcement made about him by those whom he seized. "If it is to be grasped objectively for what it shows itself to be, the Christ-form demands of those who encounter it that they accompany it through all its dimensions."[11]

We will begin, then, with a look at the first company of men who encountered him.

CONCERNING THE METHOD

Before delving into the story, it would be useful to recall our previous remarks[12] on the importance of method in facing the object. Indeed, how to approach the testimony of such an exceptional encounter is a problem which highlights in an emblematic way whether or not our entire intellectual attitude is adequate. Let us reiterate: "Method is no more than a description of reasonableness in relation to the object. The method establishes the adequate reasons with which to take steps towards the knowledge of the object."[13]

We have established that the object does not consist of a list of propositions nor does it have the plausibility of a news report. It is rather the truthful testimony about a living person who claimed to be the destiny of the world, the mystery that penetrated and became part of history. The unique nature of this claim should be kept in mind.

a) *Syntony with the Object in Time*

Here we can recall the initial point we made in the first volume in this trilogy concerning existential certainty: "I will be able to be certain about you, to the extent that I pay more attention to your life, that is, that I share in your life. The signs leading to certainty become multiplied in the measure in which you pay attention to them. For example, in the Gospel, who was able to understand the need to trust that man? Not the crowd looking for a cure, but those who followed him and shared his life."[14] This is to say that in order to know an object one must be tuned to it and this requires an active disposition which is developed through time and by living with the object.

In order to see that each individual aspect in truth receives its full meaning only by its overall relationship to the whole, the "art of total vision" is required. From one arm the archaeologist can reconstruct the whole statue, and the palaeologist can reconstruct the whole animal from a single tooth. A musicologist should be able to tell, from a single fugue motif, whether it was intended as a part of a double or a triple fugue, and to guess at the rhythmical structure that the second or third theme must have had. Everyone who has listened to Bach knows that, in the classical fugue, the rhythmical arrangement is oppositional: the first theme is slow and reposeful, the second runs along swiftly, and the third contains a rhythmical hammering; and every hearer knows that this varied thematic construction is determined by the rationale of the fugue's total architecture.[15]

The application of this is immediate: "That the measure, represented and embodied by Christ, is different in quality from all others does not need demonstration but is already implicit in the phenomenon itself. Certainly, understanding of it requires 'an eye for quality,' just as the expert unfailingly distinguishes at a glance art from oleography, something of modest quality from what is good or excellent."[16]

As can be deduced from these examples, the "art of total vision," that "eye for quality" can only be attained by listening to a great deal of music, examining many paintings or, in a scientific vein, reconstructing many statues or animal fossils. This confirms that living with, that is "investing time," is a necessary condition that enables an individual to obtain that qualitative skill which produces certainty. If we want to insist on the aesthetic example, we must also recognize that only that qualitative skill can produce certainty. Von Balthasar, whom we have just quoted, stresses this again. He is intent on thwarting:

the ruling presupposition ... that only the historical-critical outlook, unprejudiced by faith, was in any position to see the truth of what happened at that time in Palestine. A consideration of the presuppositions, now generally accepted, that govern a science dealing with spiritual and artistic works would have necessarily convinced the theologians of the naiveté of such a methodological conception ... In more general terms we can say that colors, sounds, scents exist only in the sense organs that perceive them, and because this variegated world as a whole arises in living beings and spirits, we may say that the world can unfold and exhibit its objectivity precisely in the medium of subjects.[17]

But this attuning, which is obviously an encounter between a subject and reality,[18] requires time and work on the part of the subject, who wishes to fulfil this harmonization, besides a predisposition that does not preclude it in advance. "'Attuning' (*Stimmung*) is a concept which is also applicable to the sphere of the psyche. One can be tuned into and be in perfect syntony for an event."[19]

b) *Understanding the Clues: The Road to Certainty*

Let us return to the second point we made concerning the method that leads to existential certainty. "The more powerfully one is human, the more one is able to become certain about another on the basis of only a few indications ... the more one is able to perceive with certainty ... , the more one is able to trust, because one understands the reasons for believing in another ... This may be unreasonable; if there are no adequate reasons, if there are, it is reasonable ... If the only reasonableness consisted in evidence that was immediate or personally demonstrated ... man could no longer move forward because each of us would have to go through all of the processes again."[20]

A moving text by Pierre Rousselot also stresses the following: "In natural knowledge, the quicker and more penetrating the mind is, the more effectively a slight clue suffices to lead it to a certain conclusion. The same happens in the case of supernatural knowledge ... That is why an incontrovertible tradition, going back to the Gospel itself, praises those who have no need of wonders. They are not praised for having believed without reasons; that would only be reprehensible. But we see in them truly illuminated souls, capable of grasping a vast truth through a tiny clue."[21]

Even though man, in order to survive, is naturally endowed at a fundamental level with this capacity for understanding a tiny clue, it needs time and space in order to evolve. This is a gift that can lose strength, just as modern man's sense of smell has gradually weakened in contrast to his prehistoric ancestors. And this is a gift essential for understanding the "claim Jesus makes."

Jesus constantly appealed to men's understanding. He pleaded for it, and his frequent reproach was the question, "Do you not understand?" or "Have you no understanding?"

"Do you not yet believe?" was also his question to men. This faith for which he was pleading, had nothing in common with credulity. It was quite specifically the mind's approach to truth, the recognition of that truth, the assent of the convinced mind, and not in any sense a surrender of intelligence ... According to the Gospels, belief is the discovery and understanding of the truth that is proposed to us. To the child who is learning how to swim we explain that because of natural laws there is no reason to be afraid, and if he will only make a few simple movements he will be able to swim. But the child is perhaps still afraid. He shrinks back, and does not seem to believe us. But finally the moment comes when he experiences for himself [that] what he was told is really possible, after all. He believes, and now he is able to swim. In this case, it cannot be said that faith is opposed to reason.[22]

In his precise moment of need, the child who learns to swim must be able to know how to remember that he has valid reasons for trusting his instructor. He might have this instinct, but he may also not be trained to trust in his instructor. Stiffened by layer upon layer of prejudice, man's intelligence today is not sufficiently trained to engage in a series of vital processes. "For many centuries we in the West have been subject to a tradition which presumes to found knowledge of God on the depreciation of reason, on frustrating the need for rationality and intelligibility ... What the Master of the New Testament asks of us is not that we 'humiliate' our reason but that we prize it open, to understand."[23] An intelligence that recognizes the clues for discovering the existential certainty about something fundamental for its very existence is one whose horizons are wider than an intelligence that denies the possibility at the outset. "A whole symphony cannot be recorded on a tape that is too short. Naturally, the image of Christ cannot be fully 'taken in' as can a painting; ... If he is the 'Unique One,' then no universal or eternal measure suffices to measure him; essentially, he can be measured only by himself."[24] We must train our intelligence to this new and unique measure.

THE STARTING POINT

The mystery chose to enter the history of man through a life story identical to that of any other man. Thus, it made its entrance imperceptibly. No one was there to observe or record it. At a certain point, the mystery presented itself. And this event marked the greatest moment in the lives of those who encountered it, the greatest moment in all of history.

We will begin, then, from this point. However we shall not forget that when we refer to a page from the Gospel of John, none of the many scientific debates surrounding this text has been able to diminish the evidence of the original memory and announcement which have come down to us today. "In the meantime, however, the most radical verdicts have had to be modified in the light of scientific findings: the late dating, for instance, well into the second century, has had to be revised since the discovery of very early papyri, especially P 52 of about A.D. 130, and the historical value of many of the data of John is also esteemed more highly."[25]

Undoubtedly, "John's gospel finally rests on the authority of an apostle ... as the one handing down the tradition and as 'witness.' "[26] This exceptional witness urges us to remember the point at which the presence of Jesus imposes itself for the first time as the supreme question. Transcribed on one page of the Gospel of John, as if it were something extremely important written down in a notebook, is what we might call that first instant, that first tremor of the question of Christ as it was posed in history.

Until he reached the age when he began to speak in public, Jesus had lived like any other boy, closely observing the religious rites of his people. At that time, the name of John the Baptist was on everyone's lips. People spoke of him as the prophet that had been denied them for 150 years. We must remember that this prophetic phenomenon had always been an integral part of the Hebrew tradition. And, at long last, John the Baptist, "the baptizer," interrupted what people saw as a life of disconcerting drought. From all over Judaea and Galilee, they flocked to hear him speak. Today we would say he was the object of something akin to a pilgrimage. Even Jesus went to see him.

I have said that the page on which this fact is recorded is very similar to a page in a notebook. One jots down a phrase; perhaps incompletely, and this note is the synthesis of an infinite number of things which are presupposed. The note is intended to be a signal to an active memory to recall an influx of something already experienced. It is not intended to be like details in a novel which accompany the reader and re-create, down to the last detail, a continuity with no loose ends. The novel has a public, while the note has a user. The note is concise and, in reading it, the user imagines the unsaid between the phrases, what the period abandons to memory. And to return to Eliade once again, this is the phenomenon of memory. Memory does not retain the past in an uninterrupted sequence of

events. Rather, it registers extracts. We do not remember our child-
hood as an uninterrupted fabric, a clear continuous series of events.
We recall outstanding facts, important points which, nonetheless,
clearly suggest the development of inclinations, temperament, and
character. And, if we reflect, not even yesterday, that yesterday so
apparently close to us, remains impressed on our memory according
to the uninterrupted flow of our actions.

The page we are about to examine transmits the memory of a man
who retained, throughout his life, in his eyes and heart, the moment
when his existence was invested with and overturned by a presence.
Although he vividly cherished the memory of that moment in the
ensuing years, until he was an old man, at that moment he was
certainly not aware of the fullness and the totality of what he was
encountering. His experience can be compared to that of two people
who meet in a normal way and, without immediately foreseeing it,
then marry. It is only when they are old that they will say to one
another: "Do you remember the first time we met in the mountains?
Who would ever have imagined what was going to happen?" So it is
with this page. On it, every blank space must be filled in with develop-
ments that the writer takes for granted (John 1:35–50).

Even Jesus, then, had gone to hear John the Baptist. Let us suppose it was about mid-day and, as usual, there was a small group of
people lingering about to hear him. Jesus, who had come to listen, at
a certain point, makes a move to leave. And John, as if seized by a
prophetic spirit, cries: "Behold the Lamb of God, behold him who
takes away the sins of the world." Because his listeners are probably
used to hearing him utter such phrases, which are not always comprehensible, they do not pay much attention to them for, after all, "he is
the prophet." Somebody, however, is struck by John's cry and his
fixed stare in the direction of one person. Two people, who had
come from afar, two Galilean fishermen, who, like two countryfolk on
a visit to the city, were carefully watching the events, and realizing
who John the Baptist was looking at as he pronounced that phrase
follow him. Jesus turned, saw that they were following him and asked:
"What do you want?" They said to him: "Where do you live, Rabbi?"
Jesus answered: "Come and see." The two men went, saw where Jesus
lived, and stayed with him until the evening. It was about four o'clock
in the afternoon. The lack of logic in noting that the two stayed with
him until the evening and then, without further elaboration, making
a reference to the time at which their relationship with him began –
at four o'clock in the afternoon – is interesting.

One of the two men was called Andrew. Later, he meets his
brother, Simon, and tells him: "We have found the Messiah." Now,

although two people have gone to the home of a stranger, and spent half the day there, we are not told what they did or said. What we do know is that one of them, on returning home, tells his brother: "We have found the Messiah." There is an incredible spontaneity to this account. They remained there long enough to forget that it was the evening, the hour when their companions would be going out to fish. They stayed there and attained that certainty, which they communicated to others. What happened in between is not explained. Yet they must have done something – they would have heard him speak, asked him questions, seen him move about the house doing things, busying himself with his tasks, watched his mother prepare a meal. We are only allowed to observe them the next morning, on the beach, as they wait for the return of the fishing boats and the others who went to work without them. The first thing one of the two men says to his brother who is on the boat is: "We have found the Messiah." We can only imagine the reaction to this. However, the fact is that Andrew takes Simon to Jesus. Let us visualize Simon standing there bursting with curiosity when faced with the individual whom his brother called "Messiah," how he feels himself watched and hears the words: "You are Simon, son of John. You will be called Peter." It was a Jewish custom to give people a nickname indicating their character or an important or singular event that had happened to them. Thus, in that look, Peter found his innermost self captured, his strong and granite-like character.

The next afternoon, the fishermen were on the beach mending their nets. Jesus had decided to go to Galilee and the path he took skirted the beach. Simon and Andrew must have seen him, and they must have said to the others: "There he is. That's him walking by." And one of them, Philip, just as impulsive as his brother James, stands up and runs up the path for a closer look. Then Jesus says to him in a familiar way: "Come along with me."

And, in a rapid succession of certainties transmitted quite naturally, Philip meets Nathanael and, like the others, he too feels he must tell him: "The Messiah, the Messiah Moses promised: we have found him! His name is Jesus. He is from Nazareth. He is the son of Joseph." Nathanael is older than the others, the wise one of the company, the one who does not let anything fluster him. And he replies to Philip: "From Nazareth?! Can anything good come from that place?" for the town did not have the best reputation. "Come and see," Philip answers. When Jesus notices Nathanael's arrival, he turns to him and says: "Here is a real Israelite in whom there is no deceit." Nathanael reacts almost defensively: "How can you say that when you don't even know me?" Jesus answers: "Before Philip called you, when you were under that fig tree, I saw you." And Nathanael cried: "You are the Son of God. You are the Messiah."

Let us note well where the signs of a truthful account and its nature as memory are to be found on this page. The account neither explains nor describes. Everything is assumed. It does not choose, in a structured way, what should be recorded in the annals of history. "This is what St Augustine observed in his initial comments on the Gospel of John ... 'I dare say, brethren, that perhaps St John himself did not describe events exactly as they were but as he was able, because he was a man who spoke about God ... but he was, nevertheless, a man ... He only said what a man could say.' "[27] Walter Kasper enlightens us further:

G. Bornkamm is right to observe that ... "the Gospels do not justify either resignation or skepticism. With immediate forcefulness, they reveal to us the historical figure of Jesus, although they do it differently from historical records and accounts. Yet it is very clear that what the Gospels report of the message of Jesus is still marked by authenticity, freshness, and originality which the Church's faith regarding Easter does nothing to mar and these are characteristics that conduct us directly to the earthly figure of Jesus." That the Gospels deliver their message by means of a story and that they deliver it while they relate that story is a specific feature of their literary genre, Bornkamm sustains.[28]

This page, then, relates events with all of the force and naturalness of something that is obvious and well known for the narrator, like two friends who might say to each other: "Do you remember the day we started working together?" In this recollection, the years of working together and friendship guide the memory along, while a movie camera set up in their office would have recorded only the details of time and space. And this is the whole point: it would not have transmitted and acclaimed the same content.

That page, as it is formulated, is a testimony to something which has been valid since that time and will be as long as the sun rises over the world, now and tomorrow. It is a testimony of the profound and utterly simple way with which man understood, understands, and will understand who Christ is. They were people who never imagined that they would have followed this man out of curiosity, stayed with him until the evening, forgetting even to go to work. They were left with such an impression that they reported as the truth an affirmation that perhaps he himself made, which satisfied all of the expectations of their time. Indeed, all of the interpreters of the ancient prophecies agreed that this was the moment the prophets, especially Daniel, had predicted for the coming of the Messiah. Messianic expectation was so strong that, not only according to a current of mediaeval thought – expressed by Dante – but also according to many scholars, it probably extended beyond Israel's frontiers to penetrate the pagan world, where we find an echo of it in Virgil, too.

There is no apparent proportion between the utterly simple episode we have just recalled, between this man who invites two people home, and the ensuing certainty: "We have found the Messiah." This was a certainty that would later grip Simon, Philip, and Nathanael. They found themselves face to face with someone different from all others. All those who come into contact with him are attracted by his exceptional personality. The passing of time, perhaps, would fill in a few of the details. But the immediate impression, that first perception of his singular, distinct quality remains.

Hence, in the certainty of having found the Messiah, everything would seem to have reached a conclusion. But this is only the beginning. The second chapter of John illustrates how this certainty develops – how the first perception evolves.

5 A Profound Certainty in Time

Let us observe now how the exceptional nature of the encounter was confirmed, how an impression, albeit laden with proof, became a conviction.

THE ITINERARY OF CONVICTION

Following the initial encounters, Jesus continued to live as he always had, like everyone else, in his own home, busying himself with his daily affairs. But those three or four men who had been so struck by him, had become his friends, visited him, and fished together. The second chapter of the Gospel of John recounts an invitation to a wedding. As was the custom, the guest brought friends, and since Jesus and his mother had been invited to the ceremony, he took his group of new friends with him.

The miracle of the wedding at Cana – that strange miracle when, at the end of the meal, the water was turned into wine – is one of the incidents which indicates most clearly of all Jesus' conception of life. Any aspect of existence, even the most banal, is worthy of a relationship with him and, therefore, of his intervention.

From the standpoint of the history of religions, Judaeo-Christianity presents us with the supreme hierophany: the *transfiguration of the historical event into hierophany* ... This means something more than the "hierophanising" of Time, for sacred Time is familiar to all religions. But here it is the *historical event* as such which displays the maximum of trans-historicity ... Jesus of Nazareth is, to all appearances, in no way distinguished from his contemporaries in Palestine ... Jesus eats, digests, suffers from thirst or from the heat, like any other Jew of Palestine. But, in reality, this "historical event" constituted by the existence of Jesus is a total theophany; what it presents is like an audacious effort to save *the historical event* in itself, by endowing it with the maximum of being ... It is not for its own sake that an event is valued, but only for the sake of the revelation it embodies – a revelation that precedes and transcends it.[1]

The itinerary we are tracing is situated precisely in the space and time between what could (and can) be understood from "appearances" and what could (and can) be glimpsed behind appearances, "in reality." And, in such an itinerary, *any kind* of event is decisive or revealing, precisely because of the specific and unique characteristic of the "fact" of Jesus whose action towards what is human is realized in an extreme, detailed, and concrete manner, "endowing it with the maximum of being" and progressively revealing his own being.

The miracle of the wedding at Cana marks the beginning of Jesus' progressive self-revelation (John 2:1–12). "The marriage festivities lasted for a week according to Jewish custom, when the bride was married for the first time. Care was taken to provide enough wine, which was freely poured on such occasions. Wedding presents were customary, and were in fact demanded by right of most of the guests. The embarrassment of the hosts, as the wine ran short, is understandable."[2]

With the attentiveness and sensitivity that she had undoubtedly learned from being close to her son, Jesus' mother, Mary (who cannot have been more than fifteen or sixteen years older than he was), realizes her host's embarrassment and tells Jesus, who intervenes. The evangelist concludes his account of this episode: "and his disciples believed in him" (John 2:11). We are immediately amazed at this statement. Have we not just seen in the previous chapter that his disciples already "believed in him"? And yet, this is a psychologically perfect and precise illustration of a normal phenomenon. When we meet a person who is to be significant in our lives, there is always that first instant when we have a presentiment, when something inside us is almost forced by the evidence of an unavoidable recognition: "That's him" or "That's her." But only time and space dedicated to reiterating this evidence will bolster the existential weight of our initial impression. Only sharing life (*convivenza*) enables this impression to penetrate ever more radically and deeply within us until, at a certain point, it is absolute. "... The first disciples had acclaimed Jesus as Messiah but they did not yet fully know him ... "[3] And this road of "knowing" will be confirmed over and over again in the Gospel, that is, it will need reinforcement, for the formula "and his disciples believed in him," is repeated many times, until the end. This knowing will be a slow process of persuasion and no subsequent step will negate the prior ones – even at the beginning they had believed. From sharing his life would emerge a confirmation of that exceptional, different quality that had struck them from the first moment. In sharing his life that confirmation grows. "When man realizes inwardly and humanly what it is that *this* man expresses, he realizes that to understand him, he must believe him. And, what is more, he experiences this not as a vague eventuality, but in all its cogent evidence."[4] And we have seen how the Gospel documents that belief, embraces the itinerary of conviction through a series of repeated recognitions which must be given space and time. Here, incarnated in the Gospel testimony, is that methodological reference discussed in the previous chapter. If it is true that knowledge of an object requires time and space, there is all the more reason for this law to apply to an object claiming to be unique. Even those first to encounter this uniqueness had to follow this same road.

a) *The Discovery of an Incomparable Man*

It increasingly became the habit of that first group of men to accompany Jesus when he started speaking to people in villages, town squares, and homes. One day, he had been invited for a meal in a house. A small crowd, who were all listening to him, were gathered around the threshold (Mark 2:1–12; Luke 5:17–26). Jesus lingered, as if he found it difficult to leave those people, who were attentive to his every word. The local authorities were at the front of the crowd: even though he had only just embarked on his public itinerary, those in certain positions of authority were already alarmed. As he speaks, some men suddenly arrive on the scene, carrying a paralyzed man on a mat. They would like to approach Jesus, but too many people are in the way. Consequently they take the initiative and go around to the back of the house, climb up onto the roof and, removing a part of it to create an opening, lower the paralytic man directly into the room behind Jesus. Jesus turns and looks at the man. Just imagine how that man must have felt with Jesus' gaze upon him and to hear him say: "My child, your sins are forgiven" (Mark 2:5). The reaction of the dignitaries is immediate. No one, only God, can forgive sins. But Jesus turns his eyes from the sick man to those who are objecting and asks: "Which is easier to say, 'Your sins are forgiven' or 'Rise and walk'? So that you may know that I have the power on earth to forgive sins, I say to you, rise, take up your bed, and go home" (Luke 5:22–4). And the man did rise up, amidst the people's understandable cries of wonder.

Let us now try to imagine a small group of people – those first friends and others who joined them – who for weeks, months, years witnessed such things, the exceptional quality, the boundlessness of that personality, every day, on an ever more frequent basis. However, the repeated wonders filling his whole day are not the only striking aspect of Jesus. Things, time and space, obey him without any "magical" apparatus. He manipulates reality in a totally "natural" way, as only one who is master of reality itself. The Gospel notes that by evening he was "tired by so much healing," having exercised his power on physical reality without interruption.

Yet neither was this nor his intelligence the most striking quality, capable as it was of confusing and pinning the Pharisees' proverbial cunning to the wall. The episode of the tribute to Caesar (Matt. 22:15–22; Mark 12:13–17; Luke 20:20–6) clearly exemplifies this.

By this time, the Pharisees were engaging him in continuous diatribes, challenging him, and putting him to the test in every possible way. These discussions must have been entertaining, even for those who drew near out of curiosity. Determined to put an end to it all, the Pharisees ask him if it is lawful to pay tribute to Caesar. If Jesus had given an affirmative answer, he would have betrayed his own people. If, on the other hand, he had given a negative reply, he would have been laying himself open to an accusation by the Roman Praetor. So Jesus, taking a coin, asks them to identify the effigy on it and, when they answer that it is Caesar, he silences them: "Give back to Caesar that which belongs to Caesar – and to God what belongs to God." In this way, the solution to the dilemma was admirably and enigmatically entrusted to their freedom, which was called unexpectedly into play.

His intelligence foiled all attempts to trap him. They bring a woman to him by force, who had been caught in a flagrant act of adultery (John 8:1–11) and ask him if he thinks that the Law of Moses should be applied to her, if she should be stoned. "Jesus is in a ticklish situation: which is he to contradict, his own preaching on mercy or the clear words of the Torah? But if judgment has already been given, his position is still more dangerous. He must either take a stand against Jewish justice or – assuming that the Jews did not at that time have the right to carry out the death penalty – seem to be an anti-Roman revolutionary. This would make it a critical political question like that of the tribute money."[5]

He lets them talk, training that penetrating gaze on them which made men feel that the depths of their hearts were being laid bare.

Then he stoops and, with one hand, draws signs in the dust, as if to say: "Your words are words written in dust." His accusers think they have defeated him and insist on an answer. He straightens up and replies: "He who is without sin let him cast the first stone." We can imagine the weight of the silence that follows his words. Slowly, they all turn to go, while he remains stooped there, drawing his symbolic signs in the dust with the woman standing, rigid, before him. She is alone and overwhelmed. He asks her: "Has anyone condemned you?" And she replies: "No, no one." Then Jesus tells her: "Neither do I condemn you. Go and sin no more."

However, not even this coherent intelligence or these invincible dialectics represented the most dizzying impression made on those who regularly accompanied him. The greatest miracle, which left a deep imprint on the disciples every day, was not the healing of crippled legs, the cleansing of diseased skin, or the restoration of sight to the blind. The greatest miracle of all was that truly human gaze which revealed man to himself and was impossible to evade. Nothing is more convincing to man than a gaze which takes hold of him and recognizes what he is, which reveals man to himself. Jesus saw inside man. No one could hide in front of him, and before him the depths of conscience had no secrets. This was the case of the Samaritan woman (John 4:1–42), who, in a conversation at the well, heard him tell her life story. It was precisely this that she relayed to her countrymen as a testimony to the greatness of that man: "Come and see a man who has told me everything I ever did!" This was also the case of Matthew, the tax collector (Matt. 9:9–13; Mark 2:13–17; Luke 5:27–32), who was considered a public sinner because he served the Roman economic power. Jesus simply said to him as he passed by: "Come!" And, recognized, taken hold of, accepted, he left everything and followed him. This also happened to Zacchaeus, the senior tax collector, the most hated man in all of Jericho (Luke 19:1–10). Surrounded by a great crowd, Jesus was passing by on the road, and Zacchaeus, a small man, was curious and climbed a tree for a better look. On reaching that tree, Jesus stopped, fixed his gaze upon him and cried: "Zacchaeus!" Then he said: "Come down quickly, because I must stay at your house today." What suddenly struck Zacchaeus? What made him run joyfully home? Was he making plans for his vast wealth? Did he want to generously return his ill-gotten gains, to give half of his goods to the poor? What shook him and changed him? Quite simply, he had been penetrated and captured by a gaze that recognized and loved him for what he was. The ability to take hold of the heart of a man is the greatest, most persuasive miracle of all. "Jesus imposes himself upon the conscience. He is at home in the innermost self of others ... He does not limit himself to declaring a doctrine that is his through knowledge, that he has learned through Revelation: his concern, it might be said, is a personal affair."[6]

b) *Power and Goodness*

It is hard to find a person who is powerful, and yet truly good. In Jesus, by contrast, his witnesses were able to see that gaze, which was not only powerful and prodigious, intelligent and captivating, but also good. It seems almost impossible for such great power to be contained within the bounds of profound goodness, difficult to find such sharp intelligence with such a positive simplicity, like a child's instinctive show of affection and openness. How beautiful it is to read the Gospel and discover hints, the subtle details that reveal Jesus' capacity for tenderness, his heartfelt solidarity with all human things.

So it happens when he encounters a funeral cortège in a town and hears that the deceased is the only son of a widow (Luke 7:11–17). The woman's sorrow moves him immediately, and he tells her: "Woman, do not cry." His first gesture is an act of tenderness, and then he gives back her son alive. Neither the miracle nor the gesture revealing his profound compassion had been asked of him. He takes the initiative, in a similar way, in the episode of the woman crippled and bent for so many years that she could no longer stand up straight (Luke 13:10–17). Jesus is teaching in the synagogue. He sees her, calls her over, and heals her.

Various Gospel accounts report the attention he paid to children, his capacity to relate to them (Matt. 19:13–15; Mark 10:13–16; Luke 18:15–17). Mark, the evangelist, tells us: "People were bringing little children to him, for him to touch them." Jesus does not just make some vague gesture of blessing over them. No, he takes them in his arms, rebukes whoever would try to stop him, and then blesses them, recommending to his listeners that they adopt that attitude of positive dependence on reality natural to children, in order to gain entrance to the kingdom of Heaven. In a similar account (Matt. 18:1–11), Matthew, the evangelist, reports that Jesus drew a child to him, placed him in the middle of the group, at the centre of attention, and warned people against hurting the little ones, even one child. And he was not referring to physical harm from which most people would refrain by instinct, but to moral scandal, damage to one's freedom of conscience, which one is less likely to protest against. With impassioned vigilance, Jesus is concerned with this type of wound because he says later: "Your Heavenly Father does not want even one of these little ones to be lost."

Christ has a regenerating affection for all that is valuable in humanity. After working a miracle on the Sabbath (Matt. 12:9–21), the word had spread. He goes away, but many follow him, and the Gospel notes that he "healed them all" – he turned his gaze upon them, understood them, he took all of them seriously. And the evangelist Matthew observes: "so that he fulfilled what was told by the prophet Isaiah ... '(The Messiah) will not break the crushed reed, or snuff the faltering wick, until he has made justice victorious.'"

Jesus accepts gladly what man can give him. He does not erect screens of any kind, either political, social, or cultural, shielding his willingness to embrace man. So it happened in an episode narrated by Luke (Luke 7:36–50). At a meal in the home of a Pharisee, a known prostitute suddenly bursts in, certainly an uninvited guest. She showers attention on Jesus, provoking the host's indignation who wonders to what degree it can be said that Jesus is a prophet, considering that he accepts perfume and affection from such a woman. Jesus' reaction is immediate. He shows Simon the Pharisee that he accepted the kisses and tears of the woman as a sign of her faith in him, to which she had been able to testify, thus challenging the gossip and the comments, whereas Simon who, as the host, could easily have given Jesus water for washing his dusty feet and a kiss of friendship, had not done so: "Her many sins have been forgiven her for she has shown much love."

We need also to recall the emotion that overcomes Jesus, bringing him to tears at the death of his friend Lazarus, a mysterious emotion, yet a sign of intimate solidarity with the human heart and human affairs (John 11:1–46). "On the sad journey to the tomb Jesus too is moved by the darkness of the inevitability of death ... The short remark that Jesus began to weep is the dark precursor of his confident prayer to the Father ... It is in this sense that the Jesus of John's Gospel is one with men not impervious to their distress."[7]

And Jesus "shed tears" that evening on the Mount of Olives (cf. Luke 19:41–6) as he looked on the splendour of the temple at sunset, foreseeing his city's destruction.

A QUESTION ARISES, A CERTAINTY BREAKS FORTH

Let us continue to imagine what a confirmation each day was for those who lived alongside him. As Romano Guardini observes, Jesus appears to be superior to everyone else in every circumstance. Something about him is "mysterious," because no one had ever encountered such wisdom, ascendancy, power, and goodness. As we have said, this impression only becomes increasingly precise in those who have made a systematic commitment to share in his life: the disciples.

But this man was so much more exceptional that a paradoxical question spontaneously arose: "Who is he?" It is paradoxical because Jesus' background, his date of birth, his family, and his home were well known. The question appears first among his friends and then, much later, among his enemies, even though they too were well informed about him. It is a question which illustrates that, by oneself, it is not possible to say who he really is. One can only observe that he is different from anyone else, that he merits our complete trust, and that in following him, we experience an incomparable fullness in our lives.

His secret should be discussed as much as his life. Jesus certainly teaches with forceful power. He never hesitates in his affirmations. He never shows himself "respectful of other people's opinions." But reflection on the Gospel texts reveals that if he is announcing a mystery of which he is certain, what he is announcing is a mystery concerning himself. Who was he? There is no doubt that He was a man ... In any case, he knows what lies within man and with the same simplicity with which he describes himself as greater than David, than Solomon, than Jonah and the temple, he places himself above angels.[8]

Thus he is asked who he is. And when he answers, his friends believe him, not because it is self-evident, but because of the irrefutable signs demanding trust. His enemies, by contrast, do not accept his answer and decide to eliminate him.

The sixth chapter of John reports a dramatic and beautiful moment indicative of this dynamic (John 6:22–69). One day Jesus, who used to withdraw from the company at times to pray, was followed by a large crowd. As the hours passed, the crowd became hungry. Moved to compassion, he miraculously provided them with food. In the face of this type of miracle people's enthusiasm peaked. The Gospel tells us that they wanted to crown him king because the mentality in those days identified the Messiah with a ruler greater than David, who would have exterminated Israel's enemies and conferred upon Israel its rightful position in the world. But there was a certain group of people, called God's Poor, who proclaimed themselves open to the mysteries of God. They felt uneasy within that common mentality and continued to stress the mysteriousness of the coming of the Messiah. At that moment, Jesus seemed to confirm the desire of the people for a powerful king, as he seemed to have shown himself to be. But instead, he fled, boarded a boat, and sailed to the other side of the lake. The next day was the Sabbath and, as usual, he went to the synagogue. When the attendant shook the scroll of the Scriptures to attract the attention of those who wanted to comment on them; Jesus stepped forward, as he had done other times, for it was from within the social and religious life of his people that he expounded his new message. He unrolled the scroll and read the passage about manna in the desert, the one in which Moses prayed to God because his people were lamenting, fearing that they would die of hunger in the desert. And so God sent that strange dew that was like bread. Finishing the passage, Christ rolls up the sheet of parchment again and says: "Your fathers ate the manna in the desert and they are dead; but this is the bread that comes down from heaven; so that a man may eat it and not die." Although attracted by such declarations, the people were stunned. He had already said something similar to the Samaritan woman he met at the well – if she were to drink the water he provided, she would never be thirsty again. As he speaks, the door at the back of the synagogue opens. People who had been with him the day before, who were enraptured by him and were searching for him, enter. At that precise moment, Jesus is moved by a profound emotion. All of a sudden, it might be said, the most ingenious idea he ever had in his life as a man flashes into his mind, and takes form. He tells his audience that they have sought him out because he gave them bread but affirms that he will give them his body to eat and blood to drink. The synagogue resounds with this obviously disturbing statement, and even the protests claiming that it was paradoxical could not assuage its effect. And so the opinion-makers of the day, the politicians, the professors, the journalists of that time – that is the scribes and Pharisees – began to declare that Jesus was crazy: "This is an intolerable way of speaking." The murmuring began and spread throughout the gathering which had been so enthusiastic about him shortly before and was now prepared to rise up and exalt in his discredit, sown by the powers-that-be. However, observing the reaction of the people, Jesus continued: "In truth, I tell you: if you do not eat the flesh of the Son of Man and drink his blood, you will not have life in you." The muttering grew into a din and the general opinion spread that this declaration was absurd and that Jesus was crazy. Soon it was on everyone's lips. The Pharisees slowly cleared the synagogue and, in the shadows of the dusk, Jesus remained alone with his small group of close friends. Let us try to imagine that tension-charged moment. There was a deathly silence. Jesus himself takes the initiative and breaks it: "Do you too want to go away?" And it is here that Peter, with all the vehemence of his nature, summarizes their whole experience of certainty: "Lord, we do not understand what you say either but if we leave you, to whom do we go? You alone have words which explain, which give meaning to life."

A CASE OF MORAL CERTAINTY

Psychologically, Peter's outburst is an application of our previous observation on existential or moral certainty. Indeed, Peter's attitude is profoundly reasonable. Because they shared their lives with the exceptionality of Jesus' being and his attitudes, that small group of men could only have trusted his words. They would have had to deny evidence more persuasive than that of their own eyes: "If I cannot believe in this man, I cannot believe in anything." By sharing his life, by constantly experiencing the sensation that Jesus was exceptional, it became highly reasonable to trust in him. With the passage of time, they acquired incomparable certainty about this man.

Certainly, the flash of the exceptional in him, glimpsed by the crowds who had gone to see him out of curiosity or self interest and then went away without facing what had grazed them, could not have led to anything worthy of being called a judgment. Judgment requires facing an experience, taking into account the time of its "duration." "Looking past Christ, failing to see him is something that can occur in various ways, but all these ways have this in common – that the gaze cannot withstand looking at the form of Christ himself. It is impossible to look into his eyes and maintain that one does not see him. There is, first of all, the possibility of erecting a screen before his image, and then being convinced or convincing oneself that it cannot be removed."9

The screen placed in front of reality – the disinclination of our will – renders the real object unknowable. On the other hand, moral certainty – what is born of wide-open availability, ever-faithful with the passage of time – is the cradle of a reasonable existence. This is why, in answering the question of his friends and enemies alike: "So who are you?" (cf. Mark 4:35–41, for his friends; John 10:24, for his enemies), Jesus waited until time had made his disciples certain of their attachment and his enemies persistent in their hostility. This is to say, Jesus clarified his own mystery when men had definitively determined to recognize him or not. His final self-unveiling, also unveiled "the secret thoughts of many," as Simeon had prophesied: his final self-definition conformed to the extreme poverty of spirit of those who believed in him, and offered the final, supreme pretext to those who had already decided in their hearts to reject him: "Blessed are the poor in spirit" (Matt 5:3); "if you do not welcome the kingdom of God like a little child you will never enter in ..." (Mark 10:15).

6 The Pedagogy of Christ's Self-Revelation

Until now, we have sought to identify the psychological context and the historical moment in which, according to the Gospel texts, the "Jesus" problem arose. Jesus' behaviour and actions were so exceptional that even the evidence of his family background, his personal history could no longer define him. And so the question arose: "But who is he?" Let us return to this point. Those who first raised this question knew him well. They were his friends, in his company. They went home with him. It is precisely the emergence of this question amid such human familiarity that is symptomatic of an exorbitant problem. "But who is he?" This question the disciples asked also echoed on the lips of Jesus' adversaries when, towards the end of his life, events forced even them to ask: "How long will you keep us in suspense? Tell us where you come from, who you are?" This is the same question posed in wonder by the disciples, only this time, it is in a different tone, hostile and angry.

Let us imagine a little story, an allegory that pinpoints the origin of this great question. Let us picture a mountain village a few decades ago. It is a closed, backward village. Only a mule-track links this village with the larger town down in the valley. There is no resident doctor, but there is a village council complete with a mayor. They all live in the woods. There are a few hens, several cows, and no contact with the outside world. Then a family arrives from the city and settles in the one decent house. They are a distinguished couple with two children. Although they are very polite and kind, the whole village keeps its distance from them – they spy on them through their shutters when the family passes by. No one chats with them in the one tiny village shop, or even greets them. One day, one of the villagers happens to have a serious accident. The woman from the city is a doctor and does everything in her power to heal him. This breaks the ice and gradually, very gradually, a new familiarity grows, not so much in word as in deed. The doctor's husband also appears willing to help whenever necessary: that gentleman from the city always knows what to do when a chimney or some machine needs repairing. "He must be an engineer," the villagers decide among themselves. In the evening he would go to the village's only inn where, in a cloud of tobacco smoke, the men played cards. Previously, he stood there watching them. Now, however, to the general embarrassment of everyone, he asks if he can join them, and the men of the village discover that he is also an excellent card player. In short, in just a few weeks, the family members have become the most beloved of the village. One Sunday, while playing cards with the villagers, he interrupts the game to tell them about the time he had travelled to Tierra del Fuego. They are all ears, their cards in their hands and their pipes in their mouths, for the man speaks in a fascinating and knowledgeable way. At one point, the oldest of the villagers takes his pipe out of his mouth and sets down his cards. "Listen, will you settle something we're curious about? Some of us think you're an engineer, or a scientist, while others think you're something else again. Who are you really? Why are you so good at everything and know so many things?" The man from the city replies: "Now that we really are friends I can tell you. But you must not betray me because, for a number of reasons, I am in a delicate legal position and if it were known that I was here they would come to arrest me immediately. I am the king of Portugal in exile." No one in the inn doubts the truth of this disclosure for a moment. It is evident that the answers they had anticipated were much less suited to explaining everything about that man than what he had declared. His totally unimaginable answer matched the type of person he was, conformed more to his recognizable personal qualities than their hypotheses.

Christ did not immediately and completely answer this question born in the hearts of the people who followed him, who had become accustomed to his way of speaking, his behaviour, his influence and authority over men and things. If he had, he would certainly have saved himself a death on the cross. He would not have been killed because they would have judged him as a poor madman. Indeed, an answer like the one he should have given was totally beyond the conception and the powers of perception of his followers. It would have sounded more crazy than blasphemous. This is why Jesus deployed an intelligent pedagogical method to define himself slowly so as to provoke in others a gradual evolution by assimilation, by processes bound to foster conviction, through a type of osmosis.

Moreover, in the natural order of things, in life, we do nothing that is not made up of infinitesimal steps. The best type of education is formulated in such a way as to ensure that an evolution takes place without the person who must take the step realizing it. The less confrontation, the more normal the development. Would a stomach develop healthily if it were subject, every day, to the trauma of indigestion? Anything not attained through evolution is not assimilated. Even a definition must reflect the experience of an acquisition. Otherwise, it would prove to be a schematic imposition.

Thus, if Jesus had rapidly and explicitly defined his nature as divine, he would have sparked a reaction in everyone prohibiting any possibility of trust. The Jews were too heavily monotheistic to tolerate, without appropriate preparation, any declaration that would mar their pure notion of God. Jesus, therefore, pursued an educational line which, at first, translated into implicit, concrete expressions the idea he would have to articulate openly in the end. The concrete (an incarnate idea) and the implicit (making something understood without abstract definitions) remain the most natural and effective educational approach. Even his closest disciples could not possibly have fully understood an immediate and direct answer to their question. Indeed, what Jesus would eventually say about himself would be recognized exclusively by means of the illustrative context of his person.

As we have said, it was necessary to share his life in order for that context to be illumined by his revelatory signs. Those who went to listen to him, out of curiosity, for entertainment, or to benefit from his miracles, those, in short, who approached him tangentially, could not have perceived those signs capable of persuading them to adhere to his word. Romano Guardini observed:

This revelation of the divinity made manifest in the living existence of Jesus, not with impetuous displays or spectacular gestures, but with the continuous, silent transcending of the limits of human possibility, with a greatness and vastness perceived at first like some natural goodness, like a natural freedom, like a simple and sensitive humanity – expressed in that marvellous name "Son of Man," which he willingly attributes to himself – reveals itself simply as a miracle ... a silent passage transcending the limits of human possibilities but much more portentous than the immobility of the sun or the trembling of the earth.[1]

THE ESSENTIALS OF THE PEDAGOGY OF CHRIST'S SELF-REVELATION

a) *The Master to Be Followed*

Jesus first asks people to follow him. His initial ways of proposing himself are thus comprehensible and acceptable, although they harbour much greater implications than people realize. When Jesus said to Andrew, John, and Simon: "Come with me," he issued an invitation they could easily understand. Now, let us try to project ourselves in time, to thirty years after that first moment, when the disciples, scattered throughout the known world, had become the founders of a totally new reality. Reflecting on their past, what great significance the first words they heard – "Follow me" – would acquire. But at the moment they heard them, their whole profound content was imperceptible.

I have already drawn an analogy with a familiar human experience. One person meets another who will eventually have an incisive significance in his life. If, after twenty or thirty years, he reflects on that first meeting, he will be surprised to think of the hidden meaning in one particular instant of his life, to recognize the content of a momentary encounter that his life story and time would gradually reveal.

b) *The Necessity of Renunciation*

But as time passes, Jesus makes his request more demanding. The call to follow him not only reflects readiness to acknowledge him as just and worthy of trust, but also the need to renounce oneself (Matt. 10:39). In a certain sense, this is obvious: in order to follow someone, we have to abandon our own position, ourselves. This is what he asked of his disciples – to follow him at the cost of forsaking their attachments to either family life or possessions. Something "strange," but not excessively so, was already implicit in this request. There were many "rabbis" at that time, for example, certain groups of the Essenes who retreated to the desert or settled on the edges of cities and whose followers abandoned everything they owned. But the profound meaning of this renunciation – the renunciation of "self" as a criterion – was destined to emerge later in the souls of those who followed him.

c) *Before the Eyes of the World*

But Jesus not only demanded that they follow him by detaching themselves from their possessions. He asked them to live "for him" in the
face of society. He also asks man to follow him in an exterior social
way (witnessing), and makes man's very worth, his salvation, depend
upon this. "So if anyone declares himself for me in the presence of
human beings, I will declare myself for him in the presence of my
Father in heaven. But the one who disowns me in the presence of
human beings, I will disown in the presence of my Father in heaven"
(Matt. 10:32). But then, no relationship is complete and true if it is
not strong enough to be revealed in public. To take an example, a
girl might have a relationship with a boy for some time until, at one
point, perhaps at her parents' prompting, she says to him: "Come to
my house. They want to meet you." As long as the boy procrastinates,
saying: "No, let's wait a while," and as long as he hesitates to acknowledge his relationship with her in front of his friends, the girl will
rightly feel insecure and uneasy. Until feelings or a relationship are
on such a footing that they can stand before the eyes of society and
assert themselves to others, it cannot be said that they are really true.
This is why the Lord insists on this process: that he be followed to the
extent of abandoning everything, and adherence to him cannot be
truly complete, even if one is detached from all things, until one
stands with him before everyone. Returning to the example of the
boy: he could well neglect all his own interests and even his family
relationships to be with his girlfriend but this still does not indicate
that the relationship is secure. At the same time, he might not yet
want his relationship to be asserted in society. However, the ultimate
proof of the truth of any human sentiment is its presentation to "the
eyes of the world," "the eyes of others."

FOR HIS SAKE: THE CORE OF FREEDOM

The steps we have outlined constitute the initial aspect of Jesus'
relationship with his followers. We will now discuss a later development. In this stage, Jesus becomes more insistent and presses his
request to its deepest core. This moment is destined to provoke a
great impression on those who follow him closely. Jesus begins to use
the formula "for my sake" with insistence. Gradually, the factors first
considered fundamental for establishing an identity are surpassed,
and a new identity takes shape whereby all the valid things one does
are such not because they are believed and judged to be so, but
because they are done for him. "For my sake." Above all, it must be

made clear that in acting "for his sake" one may well be ostracized by society, risk being in opposition to the common mentality (see, for example, Matt. 10:37 ff).

In the tenth chapter of the Gospel according to St Matthew, Jesus sends the Twelve to preach in the villages. He gives them instructions which well express this second phase of his teaching method.

And if anyone will not receive you or listen to your words, shake off the dust from your feet as you leave that house or town. Truly, I say to you, it shall be more tolerable on the day of judgement for the land of Sodom or Gomorrah than for that town. Behold, I send you out as sheep in the midst of wolves; so be wise as serpents and innocent as doves. Beware of men, for they will deliver you up to councils, and flog you in their synagogues, and you will be dragged before governors and kings for my sake, to bear testimony before them and the Gentiles ... Brother will deliver brother to death, and the father his child, and children will rise against parents and have them put to death; and you will be hated by all for my name's sake ... A disciple is not above his teacher, nor a servant above his master; if they have called the master of the house Beelzebub, how much more will they malign those of his household ... What I tell you in the dark, utter in the light; and what you hear whispered, proclaim upon the housetops. (Matt. 10:14–18, 21–2, 24–5, 27)

Realistic and serious as it was for those who heard it, the fundamental – and, on closer analysis, the most impressive – aspect of this "for my sake," is not so much the description, of the potential hostilities that Jesus' followers would face. What is most fundamental is the fact underlying that description: Jesus gradually places himself at the core of man's affection and freedom. And this becomes shocking when he goes so far as to compare himself with man's most intimate affections.

"While he was still speaking to the people, behold, his mother and his brethren stood outside, asking to speak to him. But he replied to the man who told him, 'who is my mother, and who are my brethren?' And stretching out his hand towards his disciples, he said: 'Here are my mother and my brethren! For whoever does the will of my Father in heaven is my brother and sister and mother'" (Matt. 12:46–50). He presents his person as an alternative to natural sentiments, even though "alternative" is not the right word, for it is only a description of the initial impact of this attitude of Jesus. What should be said is: he places his person at the core of these natural sentiments, the place he rightfully assumes is their true root. "Do not think that I have come to bring peace on earth; I have not come to bring peace but a sword. For I have come to set a man against his father, and a daughter against her mother, and a daughter-in-law against her mother-in-law; and a man's foes will be those of his own household. He who loves father or mother more than me is not worthy of me; and he who loves son or daughter more than me is not worthy of me ... He who finds his life will lose it, and he who loves his life for my sake will find it" (Matt. 10:34–7, 39).

Man's freedom is verified much more in the experience of relationships with what belongs to him than in a direct relationship with himself. A man would be more willing to lose himself than the person he loves. In fact, his freedom is more motivated in relationships of possession or preference. This is the point: Jesus places himself at the centre of these relationships, at the heart, the origin, without which they would not exist.

And this is what sparks the hostility to him. While he calls himself "master" and asks to be followed, one can recognize and go with him or decide not to, and there is still room for mere indifference. But when his proposal clearly claims to enter the dominion of our freedom, he is either accepted and it becomes love, or rejected and it becomes hostility.

The story of the "King of Portugal" can illustrate by way of analogy the aversion provoked by an individual who in some way asserts a central claim. One day after the "King of Portugal" had revealed his identity, in such an affectionate way, a police car drove into the village and took him away. He had been betrayed. By whom? By the mayor. But how could that be? The mayor had never been so respected and honoured than during that month when the gentleman had lived in the village! And yet, this mayor had felt – and could not accept – that he was no longer the heart and soul of the village. He realized that he had been replaced as the point of reference and master.

The figure of Jesus triggered a similar mechanism in terms of people's reactions to him. It was precisely because of the way he revealed himself, by beginning to manifest his presence in a claim of decisive meaning and determining power within the sphere of people's freedom, that hostility towards him began to emerge. Romano Guardini commented that a doctrine explaining life can provoke consensus or denial, but it is quite another matter when a human being advances his own claim to personify absolute importance in our lives. In order to acknowledge such a claim, the person who lends an ear to it must renounce himself, sacrifice the autonomy of his own criterion and he must do so in such an appreciable way, as only happens through love. If an individual rejects this self-renunciation, then a fundamental aversion sets in, seeking justification in every possible way. The apostles' choice became more radical precisely in this second phase as the others drew away from Jesus.

C. Tresmontant discusses this resistance in the following way:

If we study the case of Jesus of Nazareth, we can see that the resistance arose because, by his actions and his words, Jesus imparts a doctrine which rocks and overturns acquired habits, acquired representations, preconceptions. Those who transmit preconceptions and safeguard them rebel against this teacher of a new lesson. It is intolerable for them. It was intolerable then and it is so today. It always will be intolerable.

What is the explanation for this resistance to what is new, this resistance by humanity to regenerating information, this innate nostalgia for the past, for the ancient, for the primitive? One hypothesis might be that if an animal, forced to endure metamorphosis in order to reach adult form, were to be aware, and reflect on its old form, its present form and the invitation to undergo metamorphosis, it is possible that it would resist the metamorphosis with all its strength. The worm would prefer to stay a worm and the chrysalis a chrysalis rather than endure the transformation that would make the larva a different animal. It is highly possible that this is also true for man. Man is essentially an incomplete animal, called by God the Creator to a supernatural destiny, to participation in the life of God and he can only accede to this destiny through a re-birth, a transformation ... This deifiable animal – as Gregory Nazianzen described man – resists this transformation with all its strength, he resists this re-birth, this metamorphosis; and he persecutes those who call upon him to undergo this transformation. He prefers to remain the man of old, the old man, rather than become the new man. Or more precisely, he harbours two contradictory desires: one induces him to accept this metamorphosis and the other makes him turn back, regress.[2]

But the truth remains that the fundamental discriminatory factor in the decision for or against Christ lies in the inconceivable claim his very person makes, in the absolute newness of his "nature," the unimaginable answer to the question of who he is. This is the key to a whole new self-perception and image of life.

THE MOMENT OF IDENTIFICATION

But it is in a third moment that Jesus, albeit still implicitly, addresses the question: "Who are you?"

A teacher of the Waldensian denomination once said to me: "Christ never says in the Gospel 'I am God.' He always says 'I am the Son of God.' " And I responded: "If it were ever to be found in the Gospel that Christ said: 'I am the second person of the Holy Trinity,' I would immediately say that this was fraudulent." And it would be so because he was Jewish, born at that time, of that particular social background, and he would only have used the terms of the mentality belonging to a man of that period and that social background. It is unimaginable that he would have spoken with the shrewdness of a fourth century Greek, or according to the mental processes distinguishing modern man. A Jew could not even mention the word "God" because it would have meant tainting it. The name of God – and the Pharisees insisted upon this – could only be pronounced through circumlocutions. God was identified with his word, the history of a people, which is to say with texts – the Bible, as the history of a nation, the ancestors of old. The circumlocutions a Jew would have used in those times to refer to the divinity were "the Law, the prophets, and Moses," "the Patriarchs," or "the ancients," that is to say, those who had been recognized as the vehicle, the instruments of the voice of God to the extent that whatever they uttered was the voice, the very word of God. Whatever happened in their lives constituted acts of God. "Mirabilia Dei," acts of God, had manifested themselves in the lives of Abraham and Isaac, Jacob and David.

So then, Jesus responded to the great question, "Who are you?" by attributing to himself gestures and roles which the Hebrew tradition jealously reserved for Yahweh. This was how he identified himself with God. By rendering his affirmations increasingly decisive, Jesus Christ, a Jew of a certain period in history, makes as his own attitudes those which were the reserve of the divine. He habitually attributed what was really God's alone, to himself, and he expressed this above all in three different ways.

a) *The Origin of the Law*

First of all, Jesus identified himself with the origin of the Law. The word "law" was the term the Pharisees used predominantly to indicate the divine. To say that something was according to the Law was the same as saying that it was according to God. What he was accustomed to repeat must have represented an unprecedented statement for his listeners. For example, he would say: "It was said ... But I tell you." " ... You have heard that it was said to the men of old, 'You shall not kill: and whoever kills shall be liable to judgement ... ' You have heard that it was said, 'You shall not commit adultery.' But I say ... It was also said, 'Whoever divorces his wife, let him give her a writ of dismissal.' But I say ... Again you have heard that it was said to the men of old, 'you shall not swear falsely, but shall perform to the Lord what you have sworn.' But I say to you ... You have heard that it was said, 'An eye for an eye and a tooth for a tooth.' But I say to you ... You have heard that it was said, 'You shall love your neighbor and hate your enemy.' But I say to you ... " (Matt. 5:21–2, 27–8, 31–2, 33–4, 38–9, 43–4). Jesus changed what in the Pharisee's eyes represented the divine communicated to man, thus identifying himself with the origin of the law.

b) *The Power to Forgive Sins*

Let us recall the episode of the paralytic who was healed (see p. 51). Here Jesus claims to possess the power to forgive sins, and he asserts this, not just with words, but deeds. Although people were in awe of the miracle, it pointed to something else, that power of forgiveness which is God's alone.

There can be no doubt that Jesus fulfilled his duties as a devout Jew, that he shared in worship in the synagogue and in the temple and that he prayed. However he was not devout in what was and still is considered the usual sense of the word. His piety features unprecedented, even revolutionary facets, which the devout of the day felt were scandalous and sacrilegious ... He does not fit any known model. He demands change which is targeted not only at external structures and patterns of behavior but also at ideals and fundamental orientations at the very heart of man. The unprecedented freedom with which Jesus presents himself thus raises a question: "What authority have you for acting like this?"(Mark 11:28).[3]

c) *The Ethical Principle*

Let us turn to the story of the last judgment according to the Gospel of Matthew:

When the Son of Man comes in his glory, and all the angels with him, then he will sit on his glorious throne. Before him will be gathered all the nations, and he will separate them one from another as a shepherd separates the sheep from the goats, and he will place the sheep at his right hand, but the goats at the left. Then the king will say to those at his right hand, "Come, O blessed of my father, inherit the kingdom prepared for you from the foundation of the world; for I was hungry and you gave me food, I was thirsty and you gave me drink, I was a stranger and you welcomed me, I was naked and you clothed me, I was sick and you visited me, I was in prison and you came to me." Then the righteous will answer him, "Lord, when did we see you hungry and feed you, or thirsty and give you drink? And when did we see you sick or in prison and visit you?" And the king will answer them, "Truly I say to you, as you did it to one of the least of these my brethren, you did it to me." Then he will say to those at his left hand, "Depart from me, you cursed, into the eternal fire prepared ... for I was hungry and you gave me no food, I was thirsty and you gave me no drink." Then they also will answer, "Lord when did we see you hungry or thirsty, or a stranger or naked or sick or in prison, and did not minister to you?" (Matt. 25:31–44)

And the King will give them the same answer in a negative form.

This is the last judgment, and the ethical principle is at work here – not the legislator, but rather, the origin or the nature of good. And this he is. This is so true that whoever does good without even realizing that he exists, without being aware of him, does so because he is establishing, unknowingly, a relationship with him. If an action is good because of him and bad if it excludes him, then Jesus presents himself as the discriminating factor between good and bad, not so much as a judge, but as a criterion for identification. He is the good and not being with him is bad.

While still within the realm of the implicit, this is the most powerful affirmation of Christ's awareness of his identification with the divine. For, the criterion of good and bad corresponds to the principle of all things, the ultimate source of reality. The supreme ethical source is the divine, the principle of the good coincides with what is true. Good living means serving him, following him.

"This means to live at the outset according to his precepts which are more restricting and founded on higher authority than those of Moses ... It means, moreover, living like him" (Matt. 10:37, 19–29). If we really think about them, these words are yet more extraordinary than those he uses when he forgives sins or declares himself the judge of everyone's actions on the last day. "He is the one to follow on the pathway, he is the one we shall find at the very end and he is the one we seek to love in seeking to do good."[4]

7 The Explicit Declaration

In the itinerary we have followed until now, I would like to stress the methodological aspects of how the Christian problem presents itself, the dynamism which brought it into being, because this dynamism has never changed over the whole span of history. In other words, the behaviour and attitude of this man were such that the more people stayed with him and followed him, the more they felt impelled to ask: "But what makes him the way he is?" So that at a certain point the question burst forth. In recalling the concept of moral certainty (cf pp. 40ff), we mentioned this corollary: precisely because it is fundamental for living, nature allows us to arrive at certainty about human behaviour more quickly than in the case of other kinds of certainties, through our intuition of many indications converging on one point. The more one shares another's life, the more the clues are multiplied and therefore the more capable one is of moral certainty about that person. This is how it was for Jesus. His goodness, intelligence, his tremendous introspective capacity, his prodigious power over the natural world, the naturalness of his attitude towards miracles are all indications which progressively multiply and deepen for the person who lives with him or truly pays attention to him. They are indications that leave one speechless, that provoke a question one does not know how to answer, but which must be answered.

The disciples themselves certainly sought answers. The Gospels recount an episode, for example, near Caesarea Philippi. We can try to visualize its dynamics. While walking with his disciples along a path to the sea, at a certain point Jesus notices that the road before them skirts a steep crag and, as any one of us would do, he stopped for a moment to look at it. As if a thought had suddenly struck him, he turns to his disciples and says: "Who do the people say that I am?" And they answer, "John the Baptist; but others say, Elijah; and others, that one of the old prophets has risen." And he said to them, "But who do you say that I am?" (Luke 9:18–20). And Peter, in his usual impulsive way, spoke out, probably repeating something he had heard Jesus himself say, although he had not fully grasped its significance: "You are the Christ, the Son of the living God" (Matt. 16:16). Peter had already understood the evidence on which his own opinion of Jesus was based: "If I cannot trust this man I cannot even trust myself." And Jesus looked at the steep rock before him, the rock on which the city of Philippi had been built, impregnable because of its position. He then looked at Peter and said to him: "And I tell you, you are Peter, and on this rock I will build my church, and the powers of death shall not prevail against it" (Matt. 16:17). And just a moment before he had called Peter "blessed" because Peter had not come to this realization by himself. It had been revealed to him by the Father.

Everyone tries to answer the question of the identity of Christ. Everyone is disturbed by the problem it represents because any response to this question falls short. And so they ask him: "Who are you?" He does give them an answer but, as we have seen, he offers it slowly, pedagogically, introducing it almost cautiously, so that: "the smouldering wick he will not quench" (Matt. 12:20). For the answer was too much, too disturbing for their mentality. So he led them towards the explicit answer, gradually: he identifies himself as the reason for placing their lives on the line, as the very foundation for the relationships which constitute the core of our freedom. Finally, he begins to go so far as to attribute gestures and prerogatives to himself that the Bible and the whole Hebrew tradition jealously considered to be the preserve of God. He becomes the creator of the Law, the forgiver of sins, and he identifies himself as the source of ethics.

But toward the end, his declarations become explicit. At last, Christ openly presents himself as God. But he only does so when the consciences around him have already formulated decisive opinions about him. For God tends to give value to the position our freedom has already assumed. God seconds a decision our freedom has already made and forces it to reveal more clearly what it is willing to do. When one's freedom is disinclined, when it adopts a closed attitude, everything that happens encourages it to close itself even more and vice versa. "For to everyone who has will more be given, and he will have an abundance; but from him who has not, even what he has will be taken away" (Matt. 25:29).

Thus the definitive proof of his identity will be, for his friends, a chance to affirm a closer tie to him, and for his enemies, the final pretext for eliminating him.

Let us now examine three characteristic instances where Jesus explicitly manifests himself.

THE FIRST DAWNING OF EXPLICITNESS

As his time draws near, we see that Jesus, challenging the Pharisees from morning to night, has become almost a fixture in the portico of the temple. Tensions are running high in Jerusalem because of Jesus and his presence.

Among the crowds of people, which could mean both residents and pilgrims to the feast, there is much "muttering," undercover talk. Opinions are divided; but only very summary views are given. As against a certain definite, though colorless, recognition ("he's good") there is a charge of heresy: "He is leading the people astray." In Jewish law, the punishment for leading the people astray was stoning. The expression is a strong one ... But the strongest indication of the situation in Jerusalem is given by the statement that opinion is being terrorized: the people do not dare to express their views "for fear of the Jews." This clearly refers to the theocratic authorities, operating by threats and repression.[1]

Although the first moment that Jesus explicitly manifested himself might not seem to be so to the modern reader, it was at the time. These were the last few weeks of his life, and the atmosphere in the capital was just as we have described. Until then, Jesus had always slipped out of the Pharisees' hands, evading capture. But now he made a decisive entry into Jerusalem and, in this general climate, his decision provoked the sharp reaction of his friends. The evangelists write: "Then taking him aside, Peter began to remonstrate with him ... " (Matt. 16:22). Or "Peter started to remonstrate with him" (Mark 8:32). But Jesus protests: "the way you think is not God's way but man's" (Mark 8:33; Matt. 16:23).

In Jerusalem, the diatribe reaches feverish heights, and, in a city packed with pilgrims, the spectacle of these debates attracts much attention. Jesus goes so far as to attack the Pharisees at the point of their highest competency – the interpretation of the Scriptures, whose every subtlety they knew well. "Now while the Pharisees were gathered together, Jesus asked them a question, 'What is your opinion about the Christ? Whose son is he?' They said to him, 'The son of David.' " They had a ready answer to a question about the Messiah, a theme often running through the discussions of both the Pharisees and the Scribes who, like everyone else, awaited his coming in that time. "He said to them, 'How is it then that David, inspired by the Spirit, calls him Lord, saying: The Lord said to my Lord, sit at my right hand, till I put your enemies under your feet?'" Hence, the prophecy uses the same term to indicate both God and he who was to come. "'If David thus calls him Lord, how is he his son?' And no one was able to answer him a word, nor from that day did anyone dare to ask him any more questions" (Matt. 22:41–6).

Although it had seemed that not a single word of Scripture held any secrets for them, the Pharisees' interpretative skill was not strong enough to rebut Jesus' teachings. But something definitive and solemn about his reasoning must have touched them because, from that day on, they asked him no more questions. The beginning of an explicit response had therefore been given: the nature of Christ reveals itself to be divine.

A CHALLENGE

Chapter eight of the Gospel according to John reports another moment of explicit declaration. Despite the climate of tension surrounding these debates in the temple, the Gospel frequently observes that some of the Jews listening to him "believed in him." In all likelihood, their view might have been: "But this man should not be rejected out of hand. He is saying things that are thought-provoking and he backs them up with reasons ... " Today, we would call them sympathizers.

Then John notes that in just such a circumstance, Jesus turns to the men who had sympathized with him. "If you make my word your home, you will indeed be my disciples, and you shall know the truth and the truth shall make you free" (John 8:31–2). His listeners are surprised by this statement, and cut to the quick. "Jesus' words have wounded their religious and national pride. In spite of political oppression, they think of themselves as free sons of Abraham, who have never inwardly bowed to foreign rule."[2] They therefore protest to Jesus that since they have always been free, how then can he make their freedom dependent on him? "Jesus answered them, 'Truly, truly, I say to you, every one who commits sin is a slave to sin. The slave does not continue in the house forever; the son continues for ever. So if the Son makes you free, you will be free indeed'" (John 8:34–6). Jesus uses imagery to explain his capacity to set us free: "The parable envisages a household in which there are unfree servants and a son of the master of the house. The servants or slaves eventually leave the house; the son and heir remains. Such conditions existed both in Palestine and in the Hellenistic world."[3] What he means is that he who errs is as a slave of his own limitations. A slave is not part of the family. But a son is within it and of it, a part of the family of freedom. So it is as if Jesus were saying, it will be up to the son to lead you into the house and let you enter it as free men.

Jesus will certainly have noticed the resentment on the faces of his listeners, and so he persists with his intention of provoking them, right to the final consequence: "I know that you are descendants of Abraham; yet you seek to kill me, because my word finds no place in you. I speak of what I have seen with my Father, and you do what you have heard from your father" (John 8:37–8). As the situation continues to heat up, they shout out, affirming their descent from Abraham. He adds: "If you were Abraham's children, you would do what Abraham did, but now you seek to kill me, a man who has told you the truth which I heard from God; this is not what Abraham did" (John 8:39–40). The leaders of the Jews saw this as Jesus' desire to attribute "to them a father other than Abraham ... For the Jews, Abraham was the founder of the worship of God; he recognized the creator of the world and served him faithfully ... Jesus' denial of the Jews' descent from Abraham is to them an attack on their loyalty to God."[4]

"We have one Father: God." Jesus said to them, "If God were your Father, you would love me, for I proceeded and came forth from God; I came not of my own accord, but he sent me. Why do you not understand what I say? It is because you cannot bear to hear my word. You are of your father the devil, and your will is to do your father's desires. He was a murderer from the beginning, and has nothing to do with the truth, because there is no truth in him. When he lies, he speaks according to his own nature, for he is a liar and the father of lies. But, because I tell the truth, you do not believe me. Which of you convicts me of sin? If I tell the truth, why do you not believe me?" (John 8:41–6).

Pressing home his point and his cogent accusations against them, he states clearly that "all their claims, descent from Abraham and descent from God, break against the fact that they want to kill him ... Jesus speaks and argues from a sense of complete union with God."[5] And so as the discourse ensued – those who had been sympathizers were increasingly alienated because they felt that their religious pride had been hurt. They switched sides and agreed with those who were already clashing with Jesus, accusing him of being possessed by a demon and, therefore, far removed from the God who, as he had just said, had sent him.

But Jesus is now pressing firmly along the road of his self-revelation. He rejects the accusations and makes a statement destined to aggravate and heighten the din and commotion: "I have not a demon; but I honour my Father, and you dishonour me. Yet I do not seek my own glory; there is One who seeks it and he will be the judge. Truly, truly, I say to you, if anyone keeps my word, he will never see death" (John 8:49–51). The reaction is violent. They shout at him that his affirmations confirm, beyond a shadow of a doubt, that he is indeed mad, possessed. How can he promise to save people from death? All the great men of history – Abraham, the prophets – have had to reckon with death. Such a statement constitutes scandal of the highest order, both for those people who might superficially interpret what Jesus says literally and, above all, for those who might intuit that what he was really saying was: "I solemnly declare that whoever keeps my word, keeps to something for which time and history will never be able to set limits."

"Who do you claim to be?" The way the next question is formulated already shows signs of suspicion and provocation. "Even people the Jews believed to be particularly close to God, had to share the general human lot. Thus, the final question, 'Who do you claim to be?' insinuates that Jesus is making himself equal with God ... Only God is eternally alive and the giver of life ... and Jesus is claiming for himself that his word can preserve men from death. This is an invasion of the divine prerogative and means that he is setting himself, above all human beings, alongside God."[6] But Jesus had also said, "I honour my Father," adding that he did not seek "[his] own glory," and, before he went on to make the portentous declaration in verse fifty-eight, before "developing his self-revelation into a final unsurpassable statement,"[7] he would reiterate – as if to offer one last chance to some of his listeners – his dependence on the Father, that mysterious relationship which was such that it could well have aroused the suspicion of onlookers that here was a vainglorious braggart: "If I glorify myself, my glory is nothing; it is my Father who glorifies me, of whom you say that he is your God. But you have not known him; I know him. If I said, I do not know him, I should be a liar like you; but I do know him and I keep his word" (John 8:54–5).

Are there not statements in the Gospel ... that must appear to the naturally pious mind to be shot through with the shudder of *hybris*? Not only the Greek but also the Jew must be shaken to the foundations of their truly authentic piety by such words, and whoever would cry out "Blasphemy!" at hearing them would be finally justified – except in the case of Christ. In a religious sense such claims are "unbearable." For look closely: it is not the naked God who is uttering such words, but a man, even if God is supposed to be speaking from him. He cannot shift to God the responsibility for what he is saying. For this there can only be *one* justification: that this man is acting out of obedience; that he is the most profoundly obedient of all precisely as he makes divine claims for himself. But, emphatically and decisively, this is possible solely because this man, who is obeying even as he "makes" himself into a God, is a God who is obeying even as he makes himself into a man. For the former, taken by itself, would clearly be hybris and impossible to comprehend in terms of human obedience. For the surest thing that can be said of man is that he is not God.[8]

Therefore, while an attentive soul might have intuited that "the attack on Jesus' arrogance collapses on his obedience,"[9] Jesus pushes his provocation to the maximum: "Your father Abraham rejoiced to think that he would see my Day; he saw it and was glad" (John 8:56). Any human genius harbours the prophecy of a fulfilment which the person of Christ promises to incarnate. The senselessness, the unheard of, absurd presumption of what Jesus is saying is now clear to his adversaries. He has left them disarmed in their objection: "'You are not yet fifty years old, and have you seen Abraham?' Jesus said to them, 'Truly, truly, I say to you, before Abraham was, I am.' So they took up stones to throw at him; but Jesus hid himself, and went out of the temple" (John 8:57–9). The discussion, which had begun as if to deepen the sympathy and the curiosity of the people, ends in a total, dramatic breach. Some statements cause the human soul's egocentric tendency to break out. They challenge man's reason not in the fullness of its hunger for knowledge, but as it is lived normally.[10] They are warnings and pronouncements that cannot be tolerated. "Jesus now testifies to his precedence over Abraham in a clear statement ... Jesus possesses real pre-existence ... and is included in the eternal divine being."[11]

We should observe how, if the word "reason" replaced "Abraham" and "intellectuals" was substituted for "Pharisees," all of the dialectics would be perfectly applicable to the tension of our own times between faith and worldly culture.

THE CONCLUSIVE DECLARATION

Chapter twenty-six of the Gospel of Matthew provides the third and final point of reference.

In those tumultuous last weeks, the appeals for belief multiply in the form of signs and words whose aim is to make men reflect on the urgency and uniqueness of his message. After keeping him under surveillance for a long time – following him to keep a check on his teachings – the religious leaders resolve to decree that Jesus is dangerous. He does not match the idea of the Messiah people expected. He hurls abuse at the interpreters of the law, and leads people away from the true tradition with his suspicious teachings. He could attract far too much attention among the Romans. In short, they decide to arrest him. Jesus is seized and brought before the Sanhedrin for judgment. Man's need for justice is so keen that there is no injustice which does not seek to set itself up or impose itself without at least the appearance of justice, thus demonstrating the need for it.

The Sanhedrin was the great Hebrew council which should have had the power in itself to judge and condemn Jesus. However, in the existing historical circumstance by which Judea had been made a province of the Roman Empire, important cases, such as a death penalty, had to be presented to the Roman governor. Thus, in Jesus' case, the Sanhedrin took pains to follow a formal procedure which would not leave it open to any accusation of irregularity. First was the hearing before the council, and then the charges were passed over to the jurisdiction of the Roman governor.

Before the council, Jesus was the object of many accusations trumped up by a good number of false witnesses who would, however, end up contradicting themselves. The Gospels report that a climate of general unrest reigned in the Sanhedrin which sought to level a valid charge, but took some time to find one. Then two witnesses testify: "This fellow said, 'I am able to destroy the Temple of God and to build it in three days' " (Matt. 26:61). In an evidently manipulative way, they were reducing a metaphoric expression Jesus had indeed used some days before to refer to his own person and being. As he lacked more valid arguments, the high priest urges Jesus to deny this. But the false interpretation is so evident that Jesus remains silent. The high priest is under pressure. He knows he must obtain something from him for the sake of formality and so he plays his trump card. He introduces an argument that he would never have wanted to raise, whose mere mention was so scandalous because of the blasphemy it contained. " 'I adjure you by the living God, tell us if you are the Christ, the Son of God.' Jesus said to him: 'You have said so. But I tell you, hereafter you will see the Son of man seated at the right hand of Power, and coming on the clouds of heaven' " (Matt. 26:63–4). Provoked about the testimony he had come to give, Jesus could not keep silent. And so the whole council cried out at such blasphemy and sentenced him to death.

The admission that he was the Messiah would not necessarily have implied the charge of blasphemy. By attributing to himself two famous messianic texts from the Old Testament (Ps. 110; Dan. 7:13), Jesus firmly proclaimed himself the Messiah. But by adding the phrase "Son of God" (which Jesus had used) to the title of Messiah, the Christ, the high priest alluded to a prevalent and alarming suspicion which Jesus' declaration confirmed. The Sanhedrin's gesture of indignation is the response to the modern objection that Jesus did not proclaim himself God in the Gospel, but the Son of God. Evidently the religious authorities of the time saw this expression of the man from Nazareth as identifying himself with the divine, a claim they considered as a sign of confusion between human and divine reality which justified the charge of blasphemy. Of the many people who, at that time, had declared themselves the Messiah, no one had been accused of blasphemy. On the contrary, since everyone was expecting the Messiah, the intelligent religious leaders followed a very simple verification procedure. If someone really were the Messiah, the liberator everyone was waiting for, he would obtain results and, if he were not, he would fail. Nothing would have induced the Sanhedrin to abandon this "sensible" approach for such a serious charge as blasphemy if they had not been provoked by something more, something that disturbed, called into play the very idea of God which they honoured and defended against any equivocation, against anything that could falsify and adulterate their pure conception of Yahweh.

Jesus was condemned to death before the Sanhedrin for blasphemy, and this was how the charge was explained to the Roman governor: "He has claimed to be the Son of God" (John 19:7). It was also stressed to Pilate that Jesus claimed to be the King of the Jews as well, a title liable to offend the empire's representative.

THE DISCRETION OF FREEDOM

The terms for making a decision about the Christian claim are thus presented. Every other element, even that grandiose one which follows the death of Jesus and which would constitute the testimony of many who saw him again alive, would only serve to unveil "the secret thoughts of many."

When Jesus was a child, a man called Simeon, whom the Gospel describes as "upright and devout," whose fervent desire was to see the Messiah before he died, had taken the baby in his arms when his parents, as was the custom, had brought him to the temple. And Simeon said to the child's mother that her son would be "a sign that is rejected ... so that the secret thoughts of many may be laid bare" (Luke 2:34–5). The statement Jesus makes is, simply, a fact, and facts lay bare the basic position of the human heart – whether closed or open – to the mystery of being.

The Christian problem is resolved in the same terms in which it presents itself: either we are dealing with madness, or this man, who says he is God, really is God. The problem of Christ's divinity can be reduced to this alternative, which the decision of our freedom must penetrate more than anything else. It is a decision with hidden roots bound to our attitude to reality as a whole. Our freedom is not reflected in startling choices; they are not what make our lives dramatic. Nothing is more discrete than freedom. Our spirit assumes an original position in the face of reality and only afterwards develops and becomes aware of it, especially in making decisions which have the greatest implications. In confronting the problem of Jesus Christ, the consequence of the primordial position is realized, the most intimate and original position of our conscience before the totality of beings and of Being.

There is something in me which by its nature responds to the good as does the eye to light: it is *conscience* ... One of the tendencies of the modern age is to deny radically the absolute nature of conscience, reducing conscience to a matter of temperament ... or reducing conscience to a product of history or social environment ... Here, too, we must plow our way through a tangle of sociological, psychological and historical half-truths to the elementary fact: *conscience exists!* There exists in us that supreme something, which relates to the good and which responds to the good as the eye responds to light ... But conscience is also the organ by which I manage to clarify and specify the good in a situation, by which I am able to know what is good in a given place and at a given time. The act of conscience, then, is the act by which I penetrate every situation as it arises and by which I understand what is right in a given situation and so what is good.[12]

8 Christ's Conception of Life

A PREMISE: EDUCATION IN THE MORALITY
NECESSARY FOR UNDERSTANDING

1) We do not directly realize a person's true worth, unless we see it with our eyes. What is within a person can be understood to the degree in which it reveals itself – and it reveals itself through "gestures," as if by signs. They could be compared with symptoms which, for a doctor, are manifestations of a reality not directly perceptible to his observation. The more ingenious the doctor, the more capable he is of assessing the symptoms. So, to understand and judge the value of a person by his gestures, it is necessary to have "genius," "human genius." We are dealing with a psychological capacity which is developed or fostered to a greater or lesser degree. It is composed of three factors: natural sensibility, educational completeness, and attentiveness.

2) Specifically, to verify the reliability of a fact about a moral and religious personality, it is necessary to possess moral and religious genius so as to interpret this person's gestures as significant signs in that precise sense.

Let us ask ourselves, then: What is morality? Morality is the relationship between the gesture and the conception of the totality implied in the gesture. Man always moves in a universal dimension – implicit or explicit, conscious or unconscious. The capacity we are discussing here, then, is not necessarily measured by the degree of holiness, ethical faultlessness. Rather, since the elementary relationship of the particular with the whole is at stake, this capacity is better described as the original openness of the soul, as an original attitude of willingness and dependence – not self-sufficiency; it is the desire to affirm being – not oneself.

Ethically, all of this is expressed in a lived comparison of self with an ideal which surpasses us, and therefore as humility, which lies in the effort to "improve oneself," expressed in sincere desire or at least in uneasiness at our own evil. This is the sentiment proper to one who has been created, to a dependent being, and it is the very root of religiosity. Thus, the most dramatic choice our freedom will have to make and the condition for that capacity for verification which we are discussing here is to be found in the depths of our being: it is a choice between self-sufficiency and willingness. It is a choice between that decisive nuance of closure, on the one hand – that will impede verification of the facts and, therefore, understanding, and will thus become irreligiosity – and on the other hand, a lived natural simplicity that, with time, will bear its own fruits of awareness and allow the intelligence and heart to open up to the facts.

3) In the Gospel, Jesus continuously stresses that, in order to understand him, we need what we have called "moral genius." He makes the observation that an habitual self-sufficient attitude, one that is not open, makes it impossible to perceive the revelatory value of his actions. First, there is John's tragic affirmation: "He was in the world that had its being through him, and the world did not know him. He came to his own home and his own people did not accept him" (John 1:10–11). Then come the words following the encounter with Nicodemus: "And this is the judgment, that the light has come into the world, and men loved darkness rather than light, because their deeds were evil. For every one who does evil hates the light, and does not come to the light, lest his deeds should be exposed. But he who does what is true comes to the light, that it may be clearly seen that his deeds have been wrought in God" (John 3:19–21). Thus the whole beginning of the fourth Gospel introduces the drama that Christ will live with man's conscience, and the fifth, sixth, and eighth chapters especially testify to this:

Why do you not understand what I say? It is because you cannot bear to hear my word. You are of your father the devil, and your will is to do your father's desires. He was a murderer from the beginning, and has nothing to do with the truth, because there is no truth in him. When he lies, he speaks according to his own nature, for he is a liar and the father of lies. But, because I tell the truth, you do not believe me. Which of you convicts me of sin? If I tell the truth, why do you not believe me? He who is of God hears the words of God;

the reason why you do not hear them is that you are not of God (John 8:43–7).

Two great miracles related in the Gospel of John are significant in this sense: the healing of the man born blind (John 9) and the resurrection of Lazarus (John 11:1–46). In these accounts are engraved those same attitudes freedom can assume, which represent the opposite of that willing openness we are called to foster in order to be able to judge the plausibility of Jesus' claim.

In the first account, a man is cured of blindness and, because the miraculous gesture had been worked on the Sabbath, a prescribed day of rest, the religious leaders disqualify its value, claiming it was not from God. They "oppress a man prepared to believe, exercise pressure and terror among the people closed as they are to any plausible arguments for Jesus' divine origin."[1] But the man who had been healed was not to be fooled: "Their arrogant certainty conflicts with his own experience that he was healed by Jesus and he will not relinquish his hold on this fact."[2]

The sensational resurrection of Lazarus was one of Jesus' culminating signs, such that, after seeing it, many believed. But some of the onlookers "ran to tell" the Pharisees what had happened. Accustomed to the Pharisees' dominion over them, they renounced a free comparison of the facts with their humanity and they abided by the decision of the more influential. And while in the case of the man born blind, these authorities did open a type of enquiry into the facts, when faced with Lazarus' resurrection, they immediately decided to kill Jesus.

In any case, we too feel we are understood only by people who have something of ourselves within them. If we are listening to someone, and there is nothing in ourselves that is in some way close to that person's experience, there is the risk that we will misconstrue what he is saying. Thus, in order to face Jesus' conception of morality and to evaluate the personality appearing through it, humanity is required, a possibility of human correspondence with him.

4) What we have called religious genius, that ultimate openness of the spirit, is something demanding a continual commitment from us, even if it takes its cue from each person's natural gifts. What a great responsibility education has: that capacity to understand, even if it does respond to our nature, is not spontaneous. On the contrary, the original gift of sensibility in us would be suffocated if it were treated as pure spontaneity; to reduce religiosity to this pure spontaneity is the most definitive and subtle way of persecuting it, of exalting the

fluctuating, provisional aspects bound to circumstantial sentimentality.

If this gift of sensibility for our humanity is not constantly solicited and given order, no fact, not even the most startling, will find correspondence within us. Sooner or later, we all experience that feeling of obtuse alienation from reality. This happens on one of those days when we let ourselves be led adrift by circumstances, when we have remained uncommitted to making an effort of any kind. On such a day, suddenly, things, words, and deeds, once such clear motivations, cease to be so, and, abruptly, we no longer understand them.

After three years of working miracles, one day, Jesus is asked for another. People want a sign that will overcome their freedom. However, for God, humanity is to be "called" in freedom, not forced.

"The fact that Christ 'says nothing to me' in no way prejudices the fact that, in and of himself, Christ says everything to everyone. And what is involved here is not, as in individual sciences, the mere technical adaptation to the thought-patterns and conceptual dialect of this particular branch of knowledge. What is at stake, rather, is the correspondence of human existence as a whole to the form of Christ. Not only intellectual but also existential prerequisites must be fulfilled in order that the form that makes its claim on one's total existence may also find a hearing in this total existence."[3]

HUMAN STATURE

Who is Jesus? The question was asked. And he answered it. He answered it by revealing himself through all of the gestures of his personality: "If I had not come and spoken to them, they would not have sin; but now they have no excuse for their sin ... If I had not done among them the works which no one else did, they would not have sin; but now they have seen and hated both me and my Father. It is to fulfill the word that is written in their law, 'they hated me without a cause'" (John 15:22–5).

But the most enlightening "gesture," and so the most significant "sign," is a person's conception of life, his overall, definitive sentiment towards man. Only the divine can "save" man. The true and essential dimensions of humanity and its destiny can only be preserved by he who is their ultimate meaning – which is to say, recognized, acclaimed, defended. More precisely: only the divine can define the morality of a person.

It is in the conception of life which Christ proclaims, the image he gives of the human being's true stature, the realistic way he looks at human existence, it is here where the heart, in search of its destiny, perceives the truth in the voice of Christ as he speaks. It is here where the "moral" heart discerns the sign of the Presence of his Lord.

1) *The Value of the Person*

A fundamental factor of Jesus' outlook is the existence in man of a reality superior to any other reality subject to time and space. The whole world is not as worthy as the most insignificant human person. Nothing in the entire universe can compare with a person, from the first instant of his conception until the last step of his decrepit old age. Every man possesses within himself a principle by which he depends on no one, a foundation of inalienable rights, a fount of values.

We cannot confuse value with reactions the common mentality pressures us to assume. If we do, the value of the person tends to be reduced to the prevailing terms of the mentality characteristic of our environment. On the contrary, a person has value and worth by the very fact of his existence, and no one can give these to him or take them away. Value incorporates motive, the aim of an action, "whatever it is that makes taking action worthwhile," life worthwhile. That the human person is a fount of values means that the aim of his own actions is within himself.

For all these reasons, Jesus, in his life, demonstrates a passion for the individual, an urgent desire for his happiness. This leads us to consider the value of the human person as something incommensurable, irreducible. The problem of the world's existence is the happiness of each single person. "For what will it profit a man, if he gains the whole world and forfeits his life? Or what shall a man give in return for his life?" (Matt. 16:26).

No force of energy and no paternal or maternal loving tenderness has ever impacted the heart of man more than these words of Christ, impassioned as he is about the life of man. Moreover, to listen to these radical questions Jesus poses, represents the first obedience to our own natures. If we are deaf to them, we close ourselves off from the most significant of human experiences, for we would be unable not only to love ourselves, but also others. Indeed the ultimate motive pushing us to love ourselves and others is the mystery of the "I"; any other reason is only an introduction to this one.

2) *Original Dependence*

We have said that the value of the human person thus defined is an affirmation which profoundly corresponds to our own nature. But, we might ask, what is its foundation? If we do not have a clear idea of the basis of a value, we unwittingly refuse to recognize it.

What is most evident immediately following the fact that we exist, is that before we lived we had no life. Therefore, we depend. So what is the foundation, then, for Jesus' impassioned and intransigent affirmation of the absolute value of the individual, if it did not exist before, if it surged up from the world like foam on the crest of a wave only to dissolve back into the world, if it is a phenomenon derived from the past, the effect of previous biological input destined to be consumed? How can it be that the worth and value of a person do not merely exist because of his participation in the flow of reality, like a finger that is useful as long as it is a part of the body, but is valueless by itself? Christ pinpoints a reality in man that does not derive from his phenomenological provenance, a reality which is a direct, exclusive relationship with God. It is a mysteriously personal relationship, which concerns even the most insignificant human being: "See that you do not despise any of these little ones; for I tell you that in heaven their angels always behold the face of my Father who is in heaven" (Matt. 18:10). It is the content of this relationship which represents a "treasure hidden in a field, which a man found and covered up; then in his joy he goes and sells all that he has and buys that field"; it is "the fine pearl of great value" for which a man would "sell everything he owns" in order to "buy it" (Matt. 13:44–5). It is this relationship which is the irreducible subject of a knowledge that cannot be reached by deduction: "No one knows the Son except the Father, and no one knows the Father except the Son and any one to whom the Son chooses to reveal him" (Matt. 11:27); or: "Simon, son of Jonah, you are a blessed man! For flesh and blood has not revealed this to you, but my Father who is in heaven" (Matt. 16:17). Love, the supreme expression of man's self-consciousness and self-possession, which is to say his freedom, is also the adequate expression of this relationship: " 'Teacher, which is the greatest commandment in the Law?' Jesus said to him, 'You shall love the Lord your God with all your heart, and with all your soul, and with all your mind. This is the greatest and first commandment. The second is like it: You shall love your neighbor as yourself' " (Matt. 22:36–39). This is how the meaning of human life, the absolutely unique and personal destiny which is played out in it, depends on this absolutely unique and personal love. Jesus explains this when he speaks of the supreme criterion in the last judgment (cf. Matt. 25:31–46). This irreducible relationship has a value that is inaccessible and unassailable by any type of influence.

The "beatitudes" are a hymn to this freedom and dignity (cf. Matt. 5:1–12). But this hymn finds its confirmation and its enchanting application in that total abandonment to God which Jesus requires with incomparable tenderness and force in Matthew 6:25–34 when he sends his apostles on their mission:

And do not fear those who kill the body but cannot kill the soul; rather fear him who can destroy both soul and body in hell. Are not two sparrows sold for a penny? And not one of them will fall to the ground without your Father's will. But even the hairs of your head are all numbered. Fear not, therefore, you are of more value than many sparrows. So every one who acknowledges me before men, I also will acknowledge before my Father who is in heaven; but whoever denies me before men, I also will deny before my Father who is in heaven" (Matt. 10:28–33).

This unique relationship with God, insofar as it is recognized and lived, is *religiosity.*

In his earthly life, Jesus seems to concentrate on this problem of religiosity because if it remains undefined and unconfronted, the individual cannot possibly be saved, "preserve" himself. He would either be a slave to reactions that overcome him and rendered him violent to himself and others, or else he would be a slave of a series of different tyrants. This means that without that relationship with God, man as an individual cannot possibly have an indestructible, eternal face of his own. In other words, he could not possibly be a *person,* a protagonist in the universal design, playing, therefore, an unmistakable role in the history of the world.

It is the discovery of the *person* that enters the world with Jesus and it is passion for the person which makes Jesus the fervent messenger of each individual's dependence – unique and total – on the Father: "Our Father who art in heaven ... " Oh You who generate all of me from the most profound depths of my self (because "heaven" is the same as the most profound depths of creation, as Auguste Gratry observed in his comment on the Gospel of Matthew[4]).

Christian religiosity does not spring from a taste for philosophy, but from the dogged insistence of Jesus Christ, who saw in that unique relationship with God the only possibility of safeguarding the value of the individual. Christian religiosity arises as *the one and only condition for being human.* This is man's choice: either he conceives of himself as free from the whole universe and dependent only on God, or free from God and therefore the slave of every circumstance.

Jesus insisted forcefully on something which upsets the purists. This is what he was saying: listen to me, *it's worth your while.* "And if your foot should be your scandal, cut it off ... it is better for you ... if your hand should be your scandal, cut it off ... it is better for you

... if your eye should be your scandal, tear it out ... it is better for you ... " (Mark 9:45–7). The etymological derivation of the word "scandal" harbours the meaning of trap, snare. Jesus warns us not to be fooled with respect to that definitive relationship with God. This relationship or religiosity, is *worth our while* if we are to save ourselves.

We should note here that nothing is more pharisaical than tearing our garments in the face of a duty carried out with a reward in sight. Nothing is more enslaving than so-called duty for duty's sake. The coincidence of duty with happiness is probably the most concrete thing nature suggests to us, even though in an undefined way.

To conclude: the fact that the human "I" transcends the reality in which it is immersed cannot be explained by merely reducing it to that reality in which it is immersed. And on the other hand, it is evident that our "I" did not create itself. So the alternative remains: the superiority of the "I" is based on its direct dependence upon God – the principle which originates and gives everything its beginnings. Man's greatness and his freedom derive from a direct dependence on God, a condition by which man realizes and affirms himself. Dependence on God is the primary condition for what truly interests man.

"My religious relationship with God is defined by that unique phenomenon which cannot be found elsewhere, which lies in the fact that the more deeply I abandon myself to him, the more completely I let him penetrate my being, the more powerfully he, the Creator, gains authority in me, the more I become myself."[5] It is for this reason – and let us repeat – that a lived dependence on God, or religiosity, is the most impassioned directive Jesus gives in his Gospel.

HUMAN EXISTENCE

Insistence on religiosity is the first and absolute duty of the educator, that is to say, the friend, he who loves and seeks to help humanity along the pathway towards its destiny. And humanity's only point of origin is in the individual, the person. This insistence constitutes the entire calling of Jesus Christ. We cannot even think of understanding Christianity unless we begin with its origins as a passion for the individual. Jesus' understanding of humanity induces him to drive men forcefully back towards their origins, towards what will give meaning and zest to life, towards religiosity. Without that, what remains of man? *Vanitas vanitatum*: the emptiness of everything.

Religiosity, insofar as it aims to make all actions depend on God, is called morality: "Not every one who says to me, 'Lord, Lord,' shall enter the Kingdom of heaven, but he who does the will of my Father who is in heaven" (Matt. 7:21). And since the will of the Father lies in the mystery of Christ, he rightly adds, referring all things to his Presence: "Everyone then who hears these words of mine and acts on them will be like a wise man who built his house upon the rock; and the rain fell, and the floods came, and winds blew and beat upon that house, but it did not fall, because it had been founded on the rock. And everyone who hears these words of mine and does not act on them will be like a foolish man who built his house upon the sand; and the rain fell, and the floods came, and the winds blew and beat against that house, and it fell, and great was its fall" (Matt. 7:24–7).

Morality which does not begin with something greater than the "I," that is not the "I," is an ambiguity loaded with lies. To identify duty with one's own conscience is a subtle form of imposing oneself on others whereas conscience is the place where we perceive dependence, where the directive of Another emerges. Thus Jesus, a man, taught us: "I can do nothing on my own authority; as I hear, I judge; and my judgement is just, because I seek not my own will but the will of him who sent me" (John 5:30).

Only this hypothesis establishes freedom of conscience. For freedom is responsibility, that is, *to respond* to Another. And this *saves* our freedom, liberates it from identification with either an endogenous reaction or, as it always ultimately is, one induced or dictated from without by a dominant "power," and so by violence.

AN AWARENESS EXPRESSED AS ASKING

The expression of religiosity and morality inasmuch as it is conscious of its dependence on God is called prayer.

a) Prayer is the ultimate awareness of self, an awareness of structural dependence. Prayer represented the very substance of Christ's perception of himself, as we can glimpse in the beautiful chapters of John:

My Father is working still, and I am working ... Truly, truly, I say to you, the Son can do nothing of his own accord, but only what he sees the Father doing; for whatever he does, that the Son does likewise ... For as the Father has life in himself, so he has granted the Son also to have life in himself ... the works which the Father has granted me to accomplish, these very works which I am doing, bear me witness that the Father has sent me ... For I have come down from heaven, not to do my own will, but the will of him who sent me ... As the living Father sent me, and I live because of the Father, so he who eats me will live because of me ... You know me, and you know where I come from? But I have not come of my own accord; he who sent me is true, and him you do not know. I know him, for I come from him, and he sent me

... he who sent me is true, and I declare to the world what I have heard from him ... When you have lifted up the Son of man, then you will know that I am he, and that I do nothing on my own authority but speak thus as the Father taught me ... I speak of what I have seen with my Father, and you do what you have heard from your Father ... If God were your Father, you would love me, for I proceeded and came forth from God, I came not of my own accord, but he sent me ... If I glorify myself, my glory is nothing; it is my Father who glorifies me, of whom you say that he is your God. But you have not known him; I know him. If I said, I do not know him, I should be a liar like you; but I do know him and I keep his word (John 5:17, 19, 26, 36; 6:38, 57; 7:28; 8:28, 38, 42, 54).

It is the fathomless depth of this belonging, this total dependence that pervaded the situations the Gospel cites so often: "And after he had dismissed the crowds he went up into the hills by himself to pray. When evening came, he was there alone" (Matt. 14:23). But it is in the continuity of this praying – the "need to pray continually" (Luke 18:1) – in the clear awareness of this uninterrupted source of being that Jesus was able to say: "he who sent me is with me; he has not left me alone, for I always do what is pleasing to him" (John 8:16–29).

This insistence on prayer resounds in the chapters on the Last Supper. And the final prayer is the one which would synthesize the luminous and mysterious content of the conscious, continuous bond between Jesus and the Father: "All I have is yours and all you have is mine ... " (John 17:10).

b) We learn from Jesus that in prayer, human existence is revived and assumes consistency. To realize our original dependence does not mean merely to become aware of the past, of the act by which we were created. Rather, man's dependence is continuous, regards every instant, every nuance of his actions. Every fragment of our existence has its total origin in the mystery of Being – God is our true father, the father of that continuous generation that constitutes our existing. Precisely because he was able to say: "The Father and I are one" (John 10:30), he was also able to affirm: "Without me you can do nothing" (John 15:5).

Thus we arrive at the assertion that not only did man not exist before, but he would not exist now if he depended on himself. In not one moment is man self-made. If consciousness is what makes man transparent to himself, consciousness of self leads him to the conclusion that at every single moment in time, he is made by Another, His "I" is Another who makes him. Even if man were to continue his self-analysis ad infinitum, he would always arrive at this conclusion: life is pure dependence on Another. "And which of you by being anxious can add a cubit to his span of life? If then you are not able to do as small a thing as that, why are you anxious about the rest? ... For all the nations of the world seek these things; and your Father knows that you need them" (Luke 12:25–6, 30).

Life, then, expresses itself, first of all, as consciousness of the relationship with he who made it, and prayer is the realization that in "this" very moment, life is "made." Devout wonder, respect, loving subjection are all contained in this act of awareness: this is the soul of prayer. Reality perceived as fascination is the very first level of this mystical attitude, which is the most natural to man, the most elementary aspect of our awareness.

But in Jesus' example and teaching, wonder, subjection, fascination all become clear, ineffably familiar: "He was praying in a certain place and when he ceased, one of his disciples said to him, 'Lord teach us to pray ... ' and he said to them, 'When you pray, say: Father ... ' " (Luke 11:1–2). Only in the discovery of Being as love which gives of Itself continually is solitude eliminated. Existence is realized, in substance, as dialogue with the Great Presence which constitutes it – it is an inseparable companion. The company is *in* our "I." There is nothing that we do by ourselves. Every human friendship is the reverberation of the original structure of being, and if this is denied, its truth is in jeopardy. In Jesus, the Emmanuel, the "God with us," the familiarity and dialogue with him who creates us at every moment become not only a clarifying perception, but real, historical company.

"Man distinguishes himself from other creatures in that he is conscious of what he lives; this consciousness is not complete unless it reaches the Foundation from which life springs; the span of reflection does not accomplish its whole dimension unless it arrives at the Point, from which the 'I' springs forth with its gesture."[6] Therefore, prayer is not a separate act. Rather, it realizes the primary dimension of every action. The act of praying will be necessary to train ourselves to such a consciousness of every action.[7] For this reason, the height of prayer is not ecstasy, that is, such a profound consciousness of the depths that one loses the sense of the ordinary. Rather, it is seeing the depths as if they were everyday things.

How can this be explained in existential terms? "The ideal that Jesus outlined can be thus translated: 'Pray as much as you can.' This is the formula of consciousness in the face of the ideal: it is the formula of freedom in motion."[8]

c) But the complete expression of prayer is *asking*, and therefore, the original expression of human existence is asking. This is where all the dignity of consciousness and affection lies. "My food," Jesus would say in response to the disciples, "is to do the will of the one who sent me and to accomplish his work" (John 4:34).

In his relationship with the Father, Jesus' human reality was consumed in this asking and, in the prayer of the Last Supper, with all of the boundless majesty of his soul, he begged that the plan, "hidden through all the ages" (Eph. 3:9), be fulfilled: "When Jesus had spoken these words he lifted up his eyes to heaven and said: 'Father, the hour has come, glorify your Son that the Son may glorify you ... and this is eternal life that they know you the only true God, and Jesus Christ whom you have sent ... Father I desire that they also, whom you have given me, may be with me where I am, to behold my glory which you have given me in your love for me before the foundation of the world' " (John 17:1–3, 24).

In two luminous and moving passages of the Gospel, Jesus has forcefully defined the nature of prayer, which is asking, as a gesture of supreme realism towards the human condition. Here is the first:

Which of you who has a friend will go to him at midnight and say to him, "Friend, lend me three loaves, for a friend of mine has arrived on a journey and I have nothing to set before him"; and he will answer from within, "Do not bother me; the door is now shut, and my children are with me in bed; I cannot get up and give you anything." I tell you, though he will not get up and give him anything because he is his friend, yet because of his importunity he will rise and give him what he needs. And I tell you, ask, and it will be given you, seek, and you will find; knock, and it will be open to you. For everyone who seeks finds, and to him who knocks it will be opened. What father among you, if his son asks for a fish, will instead of a fish give him a serpent; or if he asks for an egg, will give him a scorpion? If you then, who are evil, know how to give good gifts to your children, how much more will the heavenly Father give the Holy Spirit to those who ask him! (Luke 11:5–13)

And here is the second. Its form is more impassioned, although it is the same request for man to live his life begging, sure of a merciful response:

He said, "In a certain city there was a judge who neither feared God nor regarded man; and there was a widow in that city who kept coming to him and saying, 'Vindicate me against my adversary.' For a while he refused; but afterward he said to himself, 'though I neither fear God nor regard man, yet because this widow bothers me, I will vindicate her, or she will wear me out by her continual pleading.' And the Lord said, 'Hear what the unrighteous judge says. And will not God vindicate his elect, who cry to him day and night? Will he delay long over them? I tell you, he will vindicate them speedily. Nevertheless, when the Son of Man comes, will he find faith on earth?" (Luke 18: 1–8).

The last terrible question defines Christ's sorrow for the world. By obliterating the consciousness of total dependence and of the inevitable state of asking – which derives its substance from prayer – man loses himself, he rejects salvation.

In practice, our evident, ultimate, and total dependence in existential terms can only be translated into asking. For he who makes us, makes us *life*. Our acknowledgment of he who makes us coincides with our asking him to give us life. We are made as attraction and thirst for life. If this great awareness we are discussing is not translated into asking, it is not true awareness. Prayer is only asking, taking anything at all. The phenomenon of our need – whatever it may be – calls us back to our dependence, and this is the cue for deepening our awareness of our dependence on God. Jesus did not disregard anything that was asked of him. Therefore, it is right to ask for anything at all, with the implicit clause Jesus voiced in Gethsemane (Luke 22:42): "not my will but yours, be done." His will in fact means my completeness, supreme happiness, which is the purpose of all asking. Just as my origin is in his hands, so then is my end.

THE LAW OF LIFE

1) *The Gift of Self*

If man as a being (person) is something greater than the world, then, as one who exists (living dynamism), he is part of the cosmos. Therefore, while in the final analysis, the aim of his actions is his own completeness or happiness, in immediate terms it is to serve the whole of which he is a part. Even though the objective of the entire universe is to help man attain happiness more fully, man, as part of the world, must also serve it.

A few days before his death, Jesus announced his destiny of glory through the cross by painting the most striking picture of what awaited him: "The hour has come for the Son of man to be glorified. Truly, truly, I say to you, unless a grain of wheat falls into the earth and dies, it remains alone; but if it dies, it bears much fruit. He who loves his life loses it, and he who hates his life in this world will keep it for eternal life. If any one serves me, he must follow me, and where I am, there shall my servant be also; if anyone serves me, the Father will honour him" (John 12:23–6).

Other images used by Christ in this passage deepen our memory of his comparison with the seed. Perhaps the best remembered representation is that of the shepherd: "I am the good shepherd ... and I lay down my life for my sheep" (John 10:14). But in his message at

Capernaum, when he identifies in the bread we eat and in the cup we drink the whole reality of his Person present in the life of man, Jesus touches upon the supreme expression of his desire to give himself up: "'It was not Moses who gave you the bread from heaven, my Father gives you the true bread from heaven. For the bread of God is that which comes down from heaven, and gives life to the world.' They said to him, 'Lord give us this bread always.' Jesus said to them, 'I am the bread of life; he who comes to me shall not hunger, and he who believes in me shall never thirst ... He who eats my flesh and drinks my blood has eternal life ... For my flesh is food indeed, and my blood is drink indeed'" (John 6:32–5, 54, 55). And in the Mass we repeat the greatest of all Christ's words: "Take it and eat ... This is my body given for you" (Matt. 26:26; Luke 22:19).

Human existence unfolds in the service of the world. Man completes himself by giving of himself, sacrificing himself. The finest comment on this Christian principle are the words of Anne Vercors before the dead body of his daughter, Violaine, in Paul Claudel's *The Tidings Brought to Mary*: "Perhaps the end of life is living? And perhaps the children of God remain sure-footed on this wretched earth? Not living, but dying – and giving in gladness all that we have. This is joy, liberty, grace, eternal youth! ... What value does the world have compared with life? And what value does life have if not to be given?"[9]

Human existence is a consuming of oneself "for" something. But what is the nature of this "consuming"? In the mystery of the Trinity, the substance of being is revealed to us as relationship. Now let us add that it is proposed to us as a gift. This is man's greatness. His life, like the Being who created him, is to be a gift: he is similar to God. Thus, man consuming himself must become gift: he is the only creature who has the capacity to be conscious of this structural element of reality.

The law of human existence is love in its dynamic reality which is offering, the gift of self. As Jesus said: "For whoever would save his life will lose it; and whoever loses his life for my sake, he will save it" (Luke 9:24). In this way, he underscores the paradoxical nature of this law: happiness through sacrifice. And the more one accepts this, the more one experiences a greater completeness already in this world. Jesus called it "peace." Thus Jesus proposes a human personality that is the result of two components: sacrifice and love. "There is no one who has left house, or brothers or sisters or mother or father or children or lands, for my sake and for the gospel, who will not receive a hundredfold now in this time, houses and brothers and sisters and mothers and children and lands, with persecutions, and in the age to come eternal life" (Mark 10:30).

A law is nothing more than the description of a stable mechanism. Man, too, as such (a being with a conscience and a will) is a fundamentally fixed mechanism. The so-called moral law describes this fundamental stability.

On what criterion will man establish this law of his action? In order to describe a mechanism, we must first consider its function, its objective. Now, since the "I" is destined for totality, its law is the giving of itself to the totality. For outside of the awareness of the totality, man will always feel imprisoned or bored.

We should note here that the goal of the human question is pursued with the means available, with "what one is." We can therefore observe two factors of human dynamism as defined by the Christian heritage: instinct and consciousness.

a) Instinct. This is what I find "already there," what determines, attracts, stimulates me. It is precisely by this that man is introduced to service to reality, by a whole series of data which he cannot avoid.

b) Consciousness. This attraction, this stimulus, this contingent impulse all have an end. Therefore, the second factor is consciousness of the proper goal of this bundle of instinctiveness. For not only does human nature possess, as a factor of its dynamism, a sense of urgency, it is also aware of the aim of this same urgency. This is to say that man, unlike animals and other things, is conscious of the relationship connecting his emerging instinct and the whole order of things. Ordering one's instinct towards the goal (which is to say, the whole) is the fundamental gift of self to the whole, the so-called "duty," whose essence, then, cannot be but love, which is self-surrender.

Chapter nineteen of the Gospel of Matthew contains perhaps the clearest explication and exemplification of this vision of man's ethical behaviour. The answer to the problem of the indissolubility of marriage has the same motivation as virginity: devotion to the "Kingdom of heaven," service to the great design. The process that nature urges "from the beginning" solicits this same gift of self to the whole that is affirmed in the radical desire for the mortification of virginity – those "who have made themselves eunuchs for the sake of the kingdom of heaven" (Matt. 19:8, 12).

But giving oneself is not human unless it is to a person. Loving is only human if one loves a person. The "whole," in the final analysis, is the expression of a person: God ("Thy will be done"). Hence, any duty is consciousness of God's will ("Thy kingdom come"). Man's acting in the world, at its most conscious level, is prayer.

In this sense, nothing is profane. Everything is collaboration, dialogue in the great temple of Being, of God. "There is a harmonization: the Gospel teaches that nothing is profane for the Christian because everything is sanctifiable. The Fathers did not neglect to stress the novelty of this. The new creation Jesus founded does not present itself under the banner of the sacred-profane counterposition. In the history of the world, God's action is a covenant which completes the fullness of creation ... "[10] Here is a similar observation, this time from Mircea Eliade: "In any case, nothing whatever, throughout the Cosmos, that is a manifestation of glory – to speak in Christian terms – can be a matter of indifference to a believer."[11]

2) *Human Disorder*

In practice, man is incapable of living, in all its completeness, the great Dependence that is his truth and its projection in life as a gift of love and service. He has a clouded conscience and an invincibly apathetic will in regard to the duty of prayer. He lives in a strange egocentric way and so, in the long term, instead of ordering himself to the whole, he strives to order the whole to himself; rather than give of himself, he strives to take for himself and instead of loving, he exploits.

This fact depends on an original, innate state. The Christian tradition attributes this to a disorder that man, through his own fault, inherits from the very origins of the human race. It determines the climate of the human world in a direction contrary to God's design: "The world was made through him, yet the world knew him not ... Now is the judgement of this world, now shall the ruler of this world be cast out ... if the world hates you, know that it has hated me before it hated you" (John 1:10; 12:31; 15:18). This is what the Christian tradition calls *original sin*. A person does not have enough energy for self-realization and the more attentive and conscious a man is, that is, the more he is capable of humanity, the more he realizes that he cannot live up to this humanity.

In his Letter to the Romans, the cry with which St Paul ends his observations is the exact same human question to which Jesus Christ is the answer: "Wretched man that I am! Who will deliver me from this body of death?" (Rom. 7:24). This cry is the only starting point which enables a man to take the proposal of Christ into serious consideration. If a man cares nothing for the question, how can he understand the answer?

To be myself, I need someone else: "Without me you can do nothing" (John 15:5). Jesus taught us that whoever accepts his message of salvation cannot avoid facing himself with sincerity, cannot avoid being realistic in his consideration of man. Alone, we cannot be ourselves. The company, which will be called the Christian community, is essential for man's itinerary. "No one comes to the Father, but by me" (John 14:6). This is the same as saying, one more time, that man cannot realize himself unless he accepts the love of Another – Another who has a precise name who, independently of your will, died for you: "Greater love has no man than this, that a man lay down his life for his friends" (John 15:13). He said this of himself: "I am the resurrection and life" (John 11:25).

3) *Freedom*

a) This redemption is not accomplished automatically. It is essential to accept the help Jesus Christ offered us and to collaborate actively with him. This happens through love that is free.

What must correspond to the free will of Christ, the man, ("For this reason the Father loves me, because I lay down my life, that I may take it again. No one takes it from me, but I lay it down of my own accord" [John 10:17]) is the freedom of the man who continually accepts him ("Light has come into the world, and men loved darkness rather than light, because their deeds were evil ... Yet you refuse to come to me that you may have life" [John 3:19; 5:40]).

b) But what is freedom?

Let us note how, particularly with regards to words that are important to their lives, men start from a pre-ordained concept or standardized image. To arrive at a definition of freedom, we must observe our own experience. When we satisfy a desire, this prompts within us an impression of freedom. It is in the total dimension of our fulfilment that freedom will be realized, according to its entire nature, as capacity for total satisfaction. Freedom is the capacity for the infinite, the thirst for God. Freedom, then, is love, because it is the capacity for something that is not us: it is Another.

c) During man's lifetime, freedom's entire goal is not attainable. Freedom is becoming. The objects freedom encounters are only anticipations, reverberations of the end. The more intense the life of freedom, the more attractive are things of any kind. But since no object is adequate to freedom's openness, it is never fully engaged. Here lies the possibility for freedom to make its choices when it is still not fully itself, because it is engaged by inadequate attractions. Now, either freedom manages to approach its end or, since it strives inexorably to attain what satisfies it the most, it stops at whatever fulfils it at a given moment, and in this way, it contradicts itself because it is made for completeness.

d) This contradiction is equivalent to the concept of evil. Whoever does evil renders himself a slave to a measure that is not the one for which he has been created (cf. John 3:20; 12:35).

e) Summarizing what the Christian inheritance teaches about the value of freedom, we can say that freedom is the capacity the conscious being possesses for complete self-realization. The course which this energy takes towards integral realization is set in motion by "things," or created beings, which, although, in a sense, contain a little of the final goal (a little of being), they have the power to attract, to solicit freedom because they represent a foretaste of partial realization. In grasping things, however, freedom is not wholly fulfilled. The attraction of things does not totally engage it. And so arises the possibility of choice. This is freedom, albeit imperfect, on its way to realization.

There may be realities which, to the free conscience, appear to possess psychologically stronger attractions than others which, in an ontological sense, are closer to the final goal. Thus, man feels "tempted," more attracted to whatever is farthest from his ultimate interest. This, therefore, places him in contradiction with himself; if he does not resist the temptation, his choice is "evil." Normally, man alone cannot resist temptation for long. Jesus Christ is the being who will continually give him back the power to choose well – to be free: "If you continue in my word, you are truly my disciples, and you will know the truth, and the truth will make you free" (John 8:31).

CONCLUSION

Jesus Christ did not come into the world as a substitute for human effort, human freedom, or to eliminate human trial – the existential condition of freedom. He came into the world to call man back to the depths of all questions, to his own fundamental structure, and to his own real situation. If certain basic values are not safeguarded, all the problems man is called to resolve in the trial of life do not dissolve, but rather become more complicated. Jesus Christ came to call man back to true *religiosity*, without which every claim to a solution of those problems is a lie. The problem of the knowledge of the meaning of things (truth), making use of things (work), human awareness (love), human co-existence (society and politics) lack a proper formulation and so, to the extent that religiosity is not at the foundation of the search for their solution, they generate ever greater confusion in the history of the individual and humanity as a whole. ("Everyone who has left houses or brothers or sisters or father or mother or children or lands, for my name's sake, will receive a hundredfold, and inherit eternal life" [cf. Matt. 19:29]). It is not the task of Jesus to resolve all the various problems, but to harken man back to the position where he can more correctly try to resolve them. This toil is a rightful part of every individual's commitment, whose function in existing lies precisely in that search for solutions.

The Christian concept of human existence foresees that the human community will never wholly adhere with its freedom to the condition to which Jesus harkens us. Therefore, the life of humanity in this world will always be sorrowful and confused. But the task of those who have discovered Jesus Christ – the task of the Christian community – is precisely to bring about, as much as possible, the solution to human problems on the basis of Jesus' call.

Jesus Christ's conception of human life, then, is essentially tension, a struggle ("I have not come to bring peace but a sword" [Matt. 10:34]). It is a pressing on, a seeking – seeking one's own completeness, one's own true "self." Nothing is more anti-Christian than a concept of life as something that is comfortable and satisfied, as a possible contingent happiness. "But woe unto you that are rich for ye have received your consolation. Woe unto you that are full!"(Luke 6:24–5).

Following Christ (faith) thus generates a characteristic existential attitude by which man walks upright and untiring towards a destination not yet reached although sure (hope). It is an attitude which is always struggling with the void of risk because the remoteness of the destination always tempts us to fall into uncertainty. This is overcome at a point beyond our own criteria – in abandonment and adherence to Jesus Christ (charity). It is this that generates a new experience of peace, the fundamental experience of life on its pathway.

9 The Mystery of the Incarnation

Throughout his public life, Jesus demonstrated his profound capacity for dominion over nature. Nature obeyed him, as a servant obeys the master of the house. And we have also highlighted how those people who were without prejudice, without preconceived hostility, inevitably stood in awe of this daily spectacle.

Let us stress this once again: Jesus' power was not sporadic. If we were to deny or remove from the Gospels the miracles Jesus worked, we would be left with almost nothing of the very fabric of his public life. Moreover, Jesus worked miracles with sovereign serenity. He needed nothing: he healed from afar, he commanded the impersonal reality of nature.

In brief, his power was manifested as something completely normal for him. Consequently, no honest man could fail to feel the same as one Pharisee who differed from the others by his sincerity. His name was Nicodemus and he came to Jesus by night and said: "Rabbi, we know that you are a teacher come from God; for no one can do these signs that you do, unless God is with him" (John 3:2). And yet at that time, the Middle East abounded in magicians and healers. But the striking aspect of the wonders Jesus performed was the way he performed them. It can be said, in synthesis, that his wonder-working responded to an ethical urgency, constituted a moral reminder, it was an education to the ideal. Because of their factiousness, his adversaries did not accept the position Nicodemus adopted, and thus they hindered themselves from seeing the facts in a simple way. For factiousness exists when a notion becomes a stance rather than an obedience to reality.

So, although as we have seen, they tried to explain away his works, give them a different meaning, they could not deny that they were exceptional. They said he was possessed, a fanatic, and a blasphemer. The authenticity of Nicodemus' interpretation, compared with that of Jesus' adversaries, depends on a freedom and sincerity of soul which permits a person to grasp the value of all the signs contained in Jesus' gestures and to accept all that ensues from them.

AN EXTRAORDINARY HISTORICAL REALITY

In retracing, then, the itinerary – from awe to conviction – of those who followed Jesus, and in hearing the answers that he gave each time to the questions arising in the hearts of those who were with him, we have been made to face the affirmation of an extraordinary historical reality: a man-God. The adversaries confront him bluntly: "We do not stone you for a good work but for blasphemy; because you, being man, make yourself God" (John 10:33). John's Gospel had already noted earlier: "This was why the Jews sought all the more to kill him, because he not only broke the sabbath but also called God his Father, making himself equal with God" (John 5:18).

1) In the Christian tradition, the origin of this fact, of this reality, is called Incarnation.

An Eastern mystic known by the name of Dionysius the Aeropagite once said: "The incarnation of Jesus under the terms of our nature is ineffable for any language and unfathomable for any intelligence ... and the fact that He assumed human substance is understood as a mystery."[1] The incarnation inasmuch as it is a divine work is a mystery. But it is particularly a mystery in terms of its result because the event that ensues from it transcends the limits of natural events. Besides accepting it as the most significant fact in the history of man, even though we cannot understand it, the task of our conscience is to develop a clear understanding of its terms, and this, on the other hand, is possible. Secondly, it is the task of our conscience to verify that it does not contradict the laws of our reason and finally, to extract enlightenment from it for a better understanding of human existence.

2) Opposition between reason and faith could therefore be reduced to the kind of opposition that originates in a mind accustomed to knowledge of certain data, but which refuses to recognize this newness of being ... requiring a renewal of reason itself ... A person who will not believe in the creation of the new, because of the hold of the familiar and the old, will also be unable to believe in the possibility of the original creation in general, or of the world or even in the possibility of his own creation, as St Justin remarked

(1 Apol. xix). This indicates an habitual fallacy of thought, which claims the right to predetermine what is possible or impossible. This is done in the name of a reality already given and long existent, as if reality had not always been subject to innovation and new creation, and consequently ... the mind would ultimately be able to acknowledge only nothingness, if its opinion were asked![2]

Taking Christ's claim seriously is a profoundly rational act, since this claim asserts itself as a fact in history, one that generates a "new being," a new creation.

3) Ultimately, the fact of the incarnation is a transcendent response to a human need which great geniuses have always been able to sense. We can perceive Giacomo Leopardi's poem, "To His Lady," as an unconscious prophecy of Christ 1,800 years after he came, a prophecy which expresses itself in a yearning to embrace that source of love intuited in the fascination with the human creature:

> Dear beauty, who art mine
> Adored, tho' ever far or veiled of face,
> Save when, a shade divine,
> Thou thrill'st the heart in sleep
> Or in the fields, if heaven
> And nature smile with some rare loveliness;
> Is it perchance that thou,
> Whose presence blessed the guileless age called golden,
> Dost flit, mere phantom now,
> Thro' ours? Or doth a grudging face hide thee
> From us, to gladden ages yet to be?
>
> I may no longer hope
> On thy true self to gaze;
> Save then it were, when naked and alone
> My soul shall reach by unfamiliar ways
> A strange, far bourne. Once, when my dim, uncertain
> Day was dawning, on this desert bare
> Methought that thou too surely must be one
> Among the pilgrims. But thy like on earth
> I found not; or if any could compare
> With thee in visage, gesture, speech, however
> Resembling thee, thine equal was she never.
>
> In valleys, where all day
> Resounds the song of the laborious hind,
> And I sit and complain

That youth's illusions will not with me stay;
And on the hills, where I in fruitless pain
Recall life's vanished hope and vanished yearnings,
One thought of thee will kindle to a fever
My sluggish blood. And in this gloomy age,
In this gross air, would I cherish ever
The lofty vision; for, since I am denied
The substance, with the shade I am satisfied.

If thou among the eternal
Ideas art numbered, which the eternal mind
Deigns not should e'er be clothed in fleshly form,
And in frail human frames
Learn with what ills our mortal life doth swarm;
Or if some other earth be mine of those
Innumerable worlds wherewith heav'n flames,
And, brighter than the Sun, the nearest star
Through kinder atmosphere above thee glows;
From here, where days are brief and skies soon darken,
To this, an unknown lover's hymn, oh hearken.[3]

Does not Leopardi's urging toward an ideal correspond with John's testimony: "which we have heard, which we have seen with our own eyes, which we have looked upon and touched with our hands, concerning the Word of life ... " (1 John 1:1)?

We could go back, perhaps, to what Henri de Lubac called "the anxious search for universality"[4] which he urged us to seek and sense in the history of the world. It is an anxious search, pervaded by the intuition that this sought-for dimension, belongs to man, yet is not his – it is a measure that man desires but he cannot determine. This immeasurable "x" for which man ultimately strives has become presence, Another. Another has become our measure. Nothing is more humanly desirable for our nature: the very life of our nature is love, the affirmation of Another as the self's meaning. H.U. von Balthasar's profound observation in this context springs to mind.

The lover does not give himself in order to fulfill himself or in order to become conscious of his own depths; he trusts in a nature which, to be sure, is in him but which nonetheless transcends him. The gesture which he makes is his own deepest gesture, but at the same time it is more than his gesture, because, through his individuality and even through his spiritual personality, the nature in him speaks and expresses itself. This law is at work not only in "first love" or in the sexual act; it leaves its impress on the family and everything belonging to it; in short, it characterizes all human life, which is a "play" of "representations" that are precisely most lively when, in the game of life, man assumes the most serious ethical responsibilities. Granted that it is he who is everywhere the focus of meaning: and yet it is not he, but a law of life and of the world which he represents, whose expression he is without his being able to equate himself with it, a law in whose affirmation he takes shelter, knowing that he will be acting best of all when he allows this great law to operate unobstructed through him.[5]

THE TERMS OF THIS NEW REALITY

1) That Jesus is a man-God does not mean that God has been "transformed into a man." Rather, it means that the divine Person of the Word possesses not only the divine nature, but also the concrete, human nature of Jesus the Man. What we call nature is identified with a type of being and what its actions manifest. If different beings make the same actions and gestures, then we infer that they share the same nature. What makes man different is the principle which is expressed with the word "I," and it is this principle – personality – which bears the stamp of nature.

The personality as principle of possession may have two natures. It is not unreasonable to think of a principle that possesses two natures, but it would be absurd to think of a mixture of two natures. What is called the mystery of the Trinity indicates that the same nature is possessed by different principles. These observations do not unravel the mystery, which remains as such, but they do show that in applying reason to the terms of the mystery, reason does not find itself contradicted.

2) Moreover, the mystery of the Incarnation establishes a method which God believed to be the right one to choose for helping man to approach him. This method can be summarized in the following way: God saves man through man.

Let us turn again to the thinking of the pseudo-Dionysius.

The Trinity, the one cause of creation ... which transcends all things, three in one, incomprehensible for our capacities of mind and which alone knows itself, has conceived the plan for our salvation ... but this salvation cannot come in any other way but through the sanctification of those who will be saved, and sanctification is the assimilation and union with God as far as possible ... The unity, the simplicity, the invisibility of Jesus, most divine Word, by means of the incarnation in our likeness, became composite, became visible ... following their goodness and love towards men and, to our greatest benefit, they have procured for us the possibility of a unifying communion with Him, marrying our misery with all that is most divine in Him even though we are inherent in Christ, like the limbs are inherent in a body, according to the nature of an immaculate and divine life.[6]

This method responds magnificently to: a) man's nature which needs sensible reality; and b) the dignity of human freedom inasmuch as God takes it on as a collaborator in his works.

3) This method is the source of knowing how to act in order to recognize God's intervention in our lives. In our seeking, we must adhere first of all to our own natures and be mindful that the outcome of our search could well demand a radical change, a breaking through and beyond the limits of our own natures. The difference between the Catholic Church and all the other Christian conceptions and interpretations springs precisely from its consideration of this method.

4) This method extends throughout history. If such an exceptional reality intervened in history, adherence to it must be possible for everyone, always: "And look, I am with you always; yes, to the end of time" (Matt. 28:20). To adhere to the method indicated by the incarnation implies that man is called to follow the same proposal of salvation at different times, in different circumstances, and by different means. If Jesus came, he is, he exists, he remains in time with his unique, unrepeatable claim, and he transforms time and space, all time and all space.

If Jesus is what he claimed to be, no time and no place can possibly have a different centre from this one.

"How, then, are we to account for the irresistible impression, felt by non-Christians especially, that Christianity is an *innovation* in relation to all previous religious life? To a Hindu who is sympathetic to Christianity, the most striking innovation (apart from the message and the divinity of Christ) is its valorisation of Time – in the final reckoning, its *redemption* of Time and of History ... Time turns into pleroma by the very fact of the incarnation of the divine Word: but this fact itself transfigures history. How could it be empty and meaningless – that Time which *saw* Jesus come to birth, suffer, die and rise again? How could it be reversible or repeatable *ad infinitum*?"[7]

INSTINCTIVE RESISTANCE

1) We have shown how reason cannot exclude outright the hypothesis that the mystery could enter the history of man as a new factor. Now that we are faced with the historical fact that this hypothesis, materialized in the person of Jesus, came to pass, we must highlight reason's possible instinctive resistance when confronted with the

annunciation of the Incarnation. It is as if man were to reject the notion that the mystery stooped so low as to become human words and deeds. Man, in all of the ages of history, resists the consequence of the mystery made flesh, for, if this Event is true, then all aspects of life, including the sensible and the social, must revolve around it. And it is precisely man's perception of being undermined, no longer being the measure of his own self, that places him in the position of refusal, on the pretext that he does not want to see the clouds lifting off the inaccessibility of the mystery obscured, he does not want to render the idea of God impure with anthropological notions, he wants freedom respected, and so on.

2) Thus, after all of the wonder at the works of Christ, undeniable and exceptional as they were, resistance to the supreme content of his message immediately made itself felt around him: "Many of the Jews who had come with Mary, and had seen what he did, believed in him; but some of them went to the Pharisees and told them what Jesus had done" (John 11:45–6). This is a typical occurrence. And, as we have said, it fulfils the elderly Simeon's prophecy to Jesus' mother in the temple. From the scribes and Pharisees then, to the scribes and Pharisees of all time, followed by their masses, the pretexts for finding his claim unbelievable will always be the same: the intolerable paradox of his humanity; his apparent failure (as the disciples were already saying at Emmaus: "But we had hoped that he was the one to redeem Israel. Yes, and besides all this, it is now the third day since this happened" [Luke 24:21]; and the wretchedness of those who followed him. And all of the philosophical considerations are thus reinforced by socio-practical observations.

The second article of the Christian symbol relates to Jesus Christ, the Son of God made man. Perhaps this is even less acceptable to pagans than the first. Celsius is clear about this: "If a few among the Christians or the Jews sustain that a God or a Son of God descended or must descend to earth, as the judge of earthly things, this is the most shameful of all their claims and there is no need for long speeches in rejecting it. What can be the sense of such a visit for God? Is it useful for knowing what is happening among men? But is it not true that God knows everything? Is he, presupposing he has divine power, incapable then of improving men without making a bodily despatch of someone to monitor the effect? Or should we put him on a par with a parvenu, unknown to the masses until then and anxious to perform for them, to flaunt his wealth? ... If, as the Christians say, he came to help men embark on the right pathway, why did he let them wander aimlessly for centuries before he realized he should do his duty?"

These are the objections of the masses but Celsius does not stop here. He raises the weight of more philosophical objections against the Incarnation.

How could it ever be imagined that there was a God who renounces, albeit temporarily, the attributes by which he is characterized?

"I am saying nothing new here but things that have been known for some time. God is good, beautiful and happy. His situation is excellent, wonderful. If he descends to man's level, it means he is subjecting himself to a change: this change will be (fatally) from good to bad, from beautiful to ugly, from happy to unhappy, from very good to very bad. Who would want to change so? Moreover, everything mortal is subject by its nature to circumstance and transformation. The immortal remains, by its essence, its identical self. It is impossible, then, that God would be subject to such a change."[8]

And it is Celsius again who raises the conclusive question: "What noble action did Christ fulfil in order to be on a par with God? Did he despise men, perhaps, did he laugh at them, did he laugh at what was happening to him? ... Why does he not seek revenge for the crime which was committed against his Father and against him?"[9]

3) In the sphere of the history of religions, the fact of the Incarnation also constitutes a divide, which the historian Mircea Eliade describes well.

Docetism, one of the earliest heresies, which was Gnostic in origin and structure, dramatically illustrates the resistance to the idea of the Incarnation. For the Docetists (the name comes from the Greek verb *dokeō*, "to seem," "to appear"), the Redeemer could not accept the humiliation of becoming incarnate and suffering on the Cross; according to them, Christ *seemed* to be a man because he had put on an appearance of the human form. In other words, the passion and death were suffered by *someone else* (the man Jesus or Simon of Cyrene).

Yet the Fathers were right in fiercely defending the dogma of the Incarnation. From the point of view of the history of religions, the Incarnation represents the last and most perfect hierophany: God completely incarnated himself in a human being both *concrete* and *historical* (that is, active in a well-defined and irreversible historical temporality) without thereby confining himself to his body (since the Son is consubstantial with the Father). It could even be said that the kenosis of Jesus Christ not only constitutes the crowning of all the hierophanies accomplished from the beginning of time but also *justifies* them, that is, proves their validity. To accept the possibility of the Absolute becoming incarnate in a historical person is at the same time to recognize the validity of the universal dialectic of the sacred; in other words, it is to recognize that the countless pre-Christian generations were not victims of an illusion when they proclaimed the presence of the sacred, i.e. of the divine, in the objects and rhythms of the cosmos.[10]

And so, defended by those who had verified its credibility by pledging their lives, the fact of the incarnation, this inconceivable Christian claim, has remained in history in its substance and entirety: a man who is God – who thus knows man – and whom man must follow if he is to have true knowledge of himself and all things.

4) The task of the Christian is to fulfil the greatest function in history – to announce that the man, Jesus of Nazareth, is God.

The theory of the incarnation was meditated, scrutinized, explored by the early fathers who elaborated its theology. Their points of departure were documents which set down in writing the facts, experiences, actions, teachings, everything concerning Jesus of Nazareth. The theologians of the centuries to follow based their work on the first-hand experience of those who had lived with Jesus of Nazareth, who had accompanied him, listened to him, observed him. This first-hand experience is the point of departure for a special science called Christology – the science which revolves around that singular person who is Jesus Christ. This science is neither deductive nor a priori. It is an inductive science which developed from an event, from an objective fact, from a first-hand experience noted down and written in the documents collated in that small library called the Books of the New Testament. These books, it should be understood, neither supplied nor conserved the first-hand experience in its entirety ... They gathered information, oral traditions, which originated ultimately from him who was the object of these traditions. In the transmission of information by word of mouth, some details were inevitably lost ... The fact remains that nevertheless, the fathers, the doctors and the theologians of the later generations had at their disposal through these little books the content of a first-hand experience, the experience of eye-witnesses. There was nothing ambiguous about this first-hand experience. Jesus of Nazareth was a man, completely and totally man, anatomically, physiologically and psychologically. But he was not just a man for he possessed a knowledge, a wisdom, a faculty, a holiness that are not of men but of the uncreated Creator, of God. Such is the initial experience.[11]

And this initial experience has an unequivocal meaning: destiny has not left man alone. It is an event which was announced throughout the centuries and which reaches us even today. The real problem at hand is that man recognize it with love.

The task of the Christian is not only the greatest, but also the most tremendous in history because it is destined to provoke unreasonable reactions; yet it is supremely reasonable to face and to verify an hypothesis on its own terms, and here the issue is precisely an event which happened in history. The struggle against the fact of the incarnation, the dogma of the Church, triggered a tenacious counter-dogma over the centuries which, presuming to be able to set the limits on God's action, proclaims that it is impossible for God to become man. From this derives the modern dogma of the whole enlightenment culture which, unfortunately, has had such a strong impact, thanks in part to its influence on the so-called Catholic "intelligentsia": the dogma of division between faith and the reality of the world with all of its problems. This attitude precisely mirrors man's childish prohibition against God intervening in his own life. This is the ultimate boundary of this idolatrous claim – the claim to attribute to God what pleases reason and what reason decides.

Notes

FOREWORD

1 Fyodor Dostoyevsky, *The Devils*, translated by David Magarshack (Middle-
sex: Penguin Books, 1971), 656.

PREFACE

1 T.S. Eliot, "Choruses from 'The Rock' VI" in *Collected Poems, 1909–1962*
(London: Faber & Faber, 1963), 177.

INTRODUCTION

1 L. Giussani, *The Religious Sense*, vol. 1, *The Giussani Trilogy*, translated
by John Zucchi (Montreal: McGill-Queen's University Press, 1997).
2 R. Callois and J.-C. Lambert, *Trésor de la poésie universelle* (Paris: Galli-
mard, 1958), 160.
3 Ibid., 162–3.
4 Gilbert Cesbron, *Il est minuit, Docteur Schweitzer* (Paris: Robert Laffont,
1952), 155: "Vous croyez pas aussi à la pensée plus forte que l'absen-
cence, n'est-ce pas?"
5 *Timaeus* 28C, translation from Francis MacDonald Cornford, *Plato's
Cosmology* (New York: Harcourt, Brace and Co., 1937), 22.
6 *Timaeus* 68D 4–7, ibid., 278.
7 Callois and Lambert, *Trésor*, 230.

8 Quoted in C. Mœller, *Sagesse grecque et paradoxe chrétien* (Paris: Casterman, 1948), 68.

9 Quoted in André Motte, "L'Expression du sacré dans la religion grecque," in *L'Expression du sacré dans les grandes religions* (Louvain-la-Neuve: Coll. Homo Religiosus, Publications du Centre d'Histoire des Religions, 1986), III: 232.

10 Ibid., III: 235.

11 Quoted in C.A. Keller, "Prière et mystique dans l'hindouisme," in *L'Expérience de la prière dans les grandes religions* (Louvain-la-Neuve: Coll. Homo Religiosus, Publications du Centre d'Histoire des Religions, 1980), 346.

12 This is clearly necessary to call to mind the sense and the value of *test* in Abraham's trial. Abraham's God is not like the deities of the Canaanites, who demanded human sacrifices.

13 Quoted in Marcel Simon, "Prière du philosophe et prière chrétienne," in *L'Expérience de la prière*, 213.

CHAPTER ONE

1 Julien Ries, *Les Chemins du sacré dans l'histoire* (Paris: Aubier, 1985), 80–1.

2 Mircea Eliade, *A History of Religious Ideas*, vol. 1, *From the Stone Age to the Eleusinian Mysteries*, translated by Willard R. Trask (Chicago: The University of Chicago Press, 1978), xiii.

3 M. Eliade, *Images and Symbols*, translated by Philip Mairet (London: Harvill Press, 1961), 20.

4 Siegfried Morenz, *Egyptian Religion*, translated by Ann E. Keep (Ithaca, New York: Cornell University Press, 1973), xv.

5 Werner Eichhorn, *Die Religionen Chinas* (Stuttgart: Kohlhammer Verlag, 1973), 163.

6 Ibid., 27.

7 J. Ries, *Il Rapporto uomo-Dio nelle grandi religioni pre-cristiane* (Milan: Jaca Book, 1983), 172–3.

8 Ibid., 113.

9 Eliade, *A History*, 1: 259–60.

10 Ries, *Il Rapporto*, 161.

11 Morenz, *Egyptian Religion*, 96.

12 Ibid., 99.

13 Ibid., 96.

14 Ibid., 106.

15 Ibid., 95.

16 W. Montgomery Watt and A.T. Welch, *Der Islam* (Stuttgart: Kohlhammer Verlag, 1980), 61.

17 Eliade, *Images and Symbols*, 55–6.

18 Ibid., 27–8.

CHAPTER TWO

1 L. Giussani, *The Religious Sense*, translated by John Zucchi (Montreal: McGill-Queen's University Press, 1997), 144.
2 J. Ries, *Les Chemins du sacré dans l'histoire* (Paris: Aubier, 1985), 83.
3 M. Eliade, *Images and Symbols*, translated by Philip Mairet (London: Harvill Press, 1961), 39–40.
4 Ibid., 40.
5 Ibid., 57–8.
6 Ries, *Les Chemins*, 73–4.
7 Eliade, *Images and Symbols*, 57–8.
8 Ries, *Les Chemins*, 72.
9 M. Eliade, *A History of Religious Ideas*, vol. III, *From Muhammed to the Age of Reforms*, translated by Alf Hiltebeitel and Diane Apostolos-Cappadona (Chicago: The University of Chicago Press, 1983), 20.
10 W. Eichhorn, *Die Religionen Chinas* (Stuttgart: Kohlhammer Verlag, 1973), 59.
11 Ibid., 64.
12 M. Eliade, *A History of Religious Ideas*, vol. II, *From Gautama Buddha to the Triumph of Christianity*, translated by Willard R. Trask (Chicago: The University of Chicago Press, 1978), 14.
13 M. Eliade, quoted in Ries, *Les Chemins*, 76.
14 Eliade, *A History*, III: 264–5.
15 M. Eliade, *A History of Religious Ideas*, vol. I, *From the Stone Age to the Eleusinian Mysteries*, translated by Willard R. Trask (Chicago: The University of Chicago Press, 1978), 372.
16 A.J. Festugière, quoted in M. Eliade, *A History*, II: 296.
17 Eliade, *A History*, I: 309.
18 Ibid., I: 305–6.
19 W. Montgomery Watt and A.T. Welch, *Der Islam* (Stuttgart: Kohlhammer Verlag, 1980), 72, 53.
20 Eliade, *A History*, III: 76; 71.
21 Ibid., II: 387.
22 Ibid., II: 386.
23 Ibid., II: 393.
24 Giancarlo Ravasi, "Introduzione," in Helmer Ringgren, *Israele* (*Storia delle Religioni*) (Milan: Jaca Book, 1987), 3.
25 Gerhard von Rad, "Some Aspects of the Old Testament World-View (1964)," in G. von Rad, *The Problem of the Hexateuch and Other Essays*, translated by E.W. Trueman Dicken (Edinburgh, London: Oliver&Boyd, 1966), 144.

26 Ibid., n.p.
27 Maurice Gilbert, "Le Sacré dans l'Ancien Testament," in *L'Expression du sacré dans les grandes religions* (Louvain-la-Neuve: Coll. Homo Religiosus, Publications du Centre d'Histoire des Religions, 1986), I: 212.

CHAPTER THREE

1 *Nostra Aetate*, 2. Conciliar Declaration on the Church's Relations with Non-Christian Religions, 28 Oct. 1965.
2 See Graham Greene, *The End of the Affair* (London: Penguin Books, 1975), 175–6.
3 Fyodor Dostoyevsky, *The Brothers Karamazov* (London: Penguin Books, 1958).
4 Sören Kierkegaard, *Journal* (Oxford: Oxford University Press, 1959).
5 L. Giussani, *The Religious Sense*, translated by John Zucchi (Montreal: McGill-Queen's University Press, 1997), 4–6.

CHAPTER FOUR

1 Rudolf Schnackenburg, *Die Kirche im Neuen Testament* (Freiburg: Herder, 1961), 13.
2 Rudolf Schnackenburg, *The Gospel According to St John*, translated by Kevin Smyth (Montreal: Palm Publishers, 1968), I: 23.
3 Vatican Council II, *Dogmatic Constitution on Divine Revelation* (1965) Ch. 5, art. 19
4 Walter Kasper, *An Introduction to Christian Faith*, (New York: Paulist Press, 1980).
5 M. Eliade, *A History of Religious Ideas*, vol. III, *From Muhammed to the Age of Reforms*, translated by Alf Hiltebeitel and Diane Apostolos-Cappadona (Chicago: The University of Chicago Press, 1983), 337.
6 Hans Urs von Balthasar, *The Glory of the Lord*, vol. I, *Seeing the Form* (San Francisco: Ignatius, 1982), 543.
7 L. Giussani, *The Religious Sense*, translated by John Zucchi (Montreal: McGill-Queen's University Press, 1997), 14–15.
8 von Balthasar, *Glory*, I: 467; 486; 487.
9 Henri de Lubac, *La Révélation divine et le sens de l'homme* (Paris: Le Cerf, 1983), 158–9; 164.
10 Ibid., 44–5.
11 von Balthasar, *Glory*, I: 459.
12 Giussani, *Religious Sense*, 12–22.
13 Ibid., 17.
14 Ibid., 20.
15 von Balthasar, *Glory*, I: 512–3.

16 Ibid., I: 451.
17 Ibid., I: 535.
18 Giussani, *Religious Sense*, 7–8
19 von Balthasar, *Glory*, I: 468.
20 Giussani, *Religious Sense*, 20, 21
21 Pierre Rousselot, *The Eyes of Faith* (New York: Fordham University Press, 1990), 35.
22 Claude Tresmontant, *Toward the Knowledge of God* (Baltimore: Helicon, 1961), 101–2.
23 Ibid., 102.
24 von Balthasar, *Glory*, I: 468.
25 Schnackenburg, *Gospel*, I: 76.
26 R. Schnackenburg, *The Gospel According to St John* (New York: The Seabury Press, 1982), III: 388.
27 de Lubac, *La Révélation*, 163–4.
28 W. Kasper, *An Introduction*, 57.

CHAPTER FIVE

1 M. Eliade, *Images and Symbols*, translated by Philip Mairet (London: Harvill Press, 1961), 169–70.
2 R. Schnackenburg, *The Gospel According to St John*, translated by Kevin Smyth (Montreal: Palm Publishers, 1968), I: 23.
3 Ibid., I: 323.
4 H.U. von Balthasar, *The Glory of the Lord*, vol. I, *Seeing the Form* (San Francisco: Ignatius, 1982), 459.
5 Schnackenburg, *Gospel*, II: 164.
6 P. Rousselot, "La Révélation du Fils," quoted in H. de Lubac, *La Révélation divine et le sens de l'homme* (Paris: Le Cerf, 1983), 185.
7 Schnackenburg, *Gospel*, II: 336.
8 Rousselot, quoted in de Lubac, *La Révélation*, 186.
9 von Balthasar, *Glory*, I: 513.

CHAPTER SIX

1 Romano Guardini, *La Figura di Gesù Cristo nel Nuovo Testamento* (Brescia: Morcelliana, 1959), 94–5.
2 C. Tresmontant, *Problèmes du christianisme* (Paris: Editions du Seuil, 1980), 250–1.
3 Walter Kasper, *An Introduction to Christian Faith* (New York: Paulist Press, 1980).
4 P. Rousselot, "La Révélation du Fils," quoted in H. de Lubac, *La Révélation divine et le sens de l'homme* (Paris: Le Cerf, 1983), 185.

CHAPTER SEVEN

1 R. Schnackenburg, *The Gospel According to St John* (New York: The Seabury Press, 1980), 2: 143–4.
2 Ibid., 2: 207.
3 Ibid., 2: 209.
4 Ibid., 2: 211; 212.
5 Ibid., 2: 212.
6 Ibid., 2: 220.
7 Ibid., 2: 217.
8 H.U. von Balthasar, *The Glory of the Lord*, vol. i, *Seeing the Form* (San Francisco: Ignatius, 1982), 478.
9 Schnackenburg, *Gospel*, ii: 221.
10 Cf. L. Giussani, *The Religious Sense*, translated by John Zucchi (Montreal: McGill-Queen's University Press, 1997), 23–33.
11 Schnackenburg, *Gospel*, ii: 223.
12 R. Guardini, *La Coscienza* (Brescia: Morcelliana, 1961), 17, 29. The author then reiterates in a note: "So that all we have said may be totally clear, I should mention the fact that by situation I mean everything concerning the person who finds himself in it ... The word of Revelation ... Christian tradition, therefore belong to it and demand evaluation ... An interpretation of a situation which precludes these elements, would not grasp reality as it is."

CHAPTER EIGHT

1 R. Schnackenburg, *The Gospel According to St John* (New York: The Seabury Press, 1980), ii: 238; 248.
2 Ibid., ii: 251.
3 H.U. von Balthasar, *The Glory of the Lord*, vol. i, *Seeing the Form* (San Francisco: Ignatius, 1982), 464.
4 Auguste Gratry, *Commentaire sur l'Evangile selon Saint Matthieu* (Paris: Tequi, 1909).
5 R. Guardini, *La Coscienza* (Brescia: Morcelliana, 1961), 52.
6 L. Giussani, *Moralità: memoria e desiderio* (Milan: Jaca Book 1980), 27–8.
7 Ibid., 29–32.
8 Ibid., 28.
9 Paul Claudel, *The Tidings Brought to Mary* (New Haven: Yale University Press, 1916), act iv, scene 5.
10 J. Ries, *Les Chemins du sacré dans l'histoire* (Paris: Aubier, 1985), 224–5.
11 M. Eliade, *Images and Symbols* (New York: Sheed and Ward, 1961), 36–7.

CHAPTER NINE

1 Piero Scazzoso, ed., *Una Strada a Dio* (Milan: Quaderni della gioventù, 1960), 63.

2 C. Tresmontant, *Toward the Knowledge of God* (Baltimore: Helicon, 1961), 116.

3 Giacomo Leopardi, *The Poems of Leopardi*, translated by Geoffrey L. Bickersteth (Cambridge: Cambridge University Press, 1923).

4 Henri de Lubac, *Catholicism, Christ and the Common Destiny of Man*, translated by Lancelot C. Sheppard and Sister Elizabeth Englund, OCD (San Francisco: Ignatius Press, 1988).

5 H.U. von Balthasar, *The Glory of the Lord*, vol. I, *Seeing the Form* (San Francisco: Ignatius Press, 1982), 445.

6 Scazzoso, ed., *Una Strada*, 38–9; 107.

7 M. Eliade, *Images and Symbols*, translated by Philip Mairet (London: Harvill Press, 1961), 169.

8 Gustave Bardy, *La Conversion au christianisme durant les premiers siècles* (Paris: Aubier, 1949), 178–9.

9 Quoted in C. Mœller, *Sagesse grecque et paradoxe chrétien* (Paris: Casterman, 1948), 20.

10 M. Eliade, *A History of Religious Ideas*, vol. III, *From Muhammed to the Age of Reforms*, translated by Alf Hiltebeitel and Diane Apostolos-Cappadona (Chicago: The University of Chicago Press, 1983), 408–9.

11 C. Tresmontant, *Problèmes du christianisme* (Paris: Editions du Seuil, 1980), 253–4.

Subject Index

Author Index